D0742247

THE MYTHS OF LIBERAL ZIONISM

THE MYTHS OF
LIBERAL ZIONISM

YITZHAK LAOR

VERSO
London • New York

English edition published by Verso 2009
© Verso 2009
First published as
Le nouveau philosémitisme européen et le "camp de la paix" en Israël
© La Fabrique 2007
All rights reserved

1 3 5 7 9 10 8 6 4 2

Verso
UK: 6 Meard Street, London W1F 0EG
US: 20 Jay Street, Suite 1010, Brooklyn, NY 11201
www.versobooks.com

Verso is the imprint of New Left Books

ISBN-13: 978-1-84467-314-8

British Library Cataloguing in Publication Data
A catalogue record for this book is available from the British Library

Library of Congress Cataloging-in-Publication Data
A catalog record for this book is available from the Library of Congress

Typeset by Hewer Text UK Ltd, Edinburgh
Printed in the US by Maple Vail

CONTENTS

FOREWORD BY
JOSÉ SARAMAGO

The importance of the analyses contained in this book can be measured against its principal objective: to disentangle an intricate ball of twine, revealing how deep contradictions within Israeli society are and how the great majority of the population seems to have decided to support the most daring positions of its government with regard to the treatment meted out to the Palestinians. This is treatment characterized, as we all know, by a contempt and an intolerance which, on a practical level, have led to the extreme of denying any degree of humanity to the Palestinian people, at times even denying their basic right to existence. When Yitzhak Laor wrote *The Myths of Liberal Zionism*,[1] it was almost impossible to foresee the day when the president of the United States would come to insist on the withdrawal of the settlements (over 200 settlements

---

1   Published first in France, in 2007, as *Le nouveau philosémitisme européen et le "camp de la paix" en Israël*.

ranging from the "legal ones," meaning those authorized and built according to the will of the government in Tel Aviv, and the "illegal ones," those to which the government turns a blind eye, inhabited, all told, by over half a million residents whose presence is the major obstacle to peace today), not to mention the recognition of the elementary right of the Palestinians to their own independent and viable state. This was something already noted by George Bush Sr, when he forced Israel to recognize that talking at one and the same time about peace and about the settlements was an irrational and inherent contradiction. Former Prime Minister Ehud Olmert seems to have been aware of this when he declared to *Haaretz*, in November 2007, that if a speedy solution and a division into the two states were not rapidly arrived at "the state of Israel would be finished." He didn't go so far as to do anything to achieve the resolution of this problem, but his words at least still resonate. They help us to comprehend how the settlers were always the sword of Damocles, suspended over the Israeli governments, and now more than ever, over the head of Binyamin Netanyahu.

José Saramago
2009

PREFACE TO THE
ENGLISH-LANGUAGE EDITION

I once visited the United States shortly after an incident in which a college student had opened fire and killed several of his fellow students on the campus of Virginia Tech. The taxi driver who took me from JFK Airport to Washington Square in New York heard I was from Israel, and therefore excitedly told me about the Israeli professor who protected his students and was shot to death. He survived the Nazi concentration camps to die here as a hero, the driver told me. I was truly impressed by this historicization, and when I spoke to my wife on the phone later that day I told her about it. She said she had heard the same description on CNN, and, indeed, I later heard the same story from President Bush, or his speech writers, on TV.

I think I know how to write about our present time and place to people who live alongside me, who use the same language, even though I belong to a political minority. I am more skeptical about my ability to talk about this time and place to outsiders. Not just because our history long ago turned into a collection of soundbites, or because it is very easy for a Hebrew writer to tell his parents' life story as a kind of illustration of the dramatic history of his people in the first half of the twentieth century, or to tell my own life story as an illustration of the dramatic history of the country I have lived in over the second half of the twentieth century. I am skeptical of my ability because I find it extremely hard to try to sharpen my questions, mainly questions about the nature of the current historical moment in Israel, the place where I was born and will probably die. Twenty years ago I wrote a poem in which I tried to explain Israeli aggressiveness thus:

> We didn't grow up where our fathers grew up.
> They didn't grow up where
> Their fathers did. We learnt not to
> Feel nostalgic (we can feel nostalgic for any tombstone
> Decided upon), we don't belong any
> Where (we shall belong easily to anything
> When demanded), we move across
> Countries, we sleep in fancy
> Hotels, we sleep in cold
> Barns, we love only in order to be

Loved, we rape only
To be remembered, we enjoy
Only so as to register ownership, destroying
Mainly villages, declaring ownership
And leaving, hating peasants, mainly
Peasants (if necessary, we'll also cultivate
The land).[1]

I didn't content myself with writing poetry, because I thought that through it I could not capture all this history which so occupies me: "We didn't grow up where our fathers grew up. They didn't grow up where their fathers did."

What in this eternal foreignness to the landscape that one's father loved in his childhood, or that one's father's father loved in his childhood, what in this foreignness is relevant to our patriotism (always abstract) and what is not? I am not sure that I have good answers. And yet I am trying to ask questions about the ability to write beyond images, beyond the simple images that the TV news chatters about.

There is something about our Israeli lives, about how we perceive ourselves and how we perceive others' perception of us, that is entirely connected to the

---

1   Published in Hebrew in my *Shieim Be-Emek Ha-Barzel* [Poems in the Valley of Iron], trans. Aloma Halter, Tel Aviv, 1989.

European origins of our concept of nationality, democracy and political structure.

Even though our Israeli lives are very dependent on the United States of America, the fact is that when we, in the heart of the Middle East, talk to our metropolis, yearn for its love, ask for its moral support and recognition of our cultural values, we are not really talking to the United States, maybe because we take its love for granted—hence we do not make any real efforts to desire its desire—but maybe we simply do not really understand or know it. And though "understanding the US" is almost a profession in Israeli journalism, and though we are very up to date with most US TV drama series, soap operas and sitcoms, even we understand that the United States is not just what we see on TV, or in Hollywood movies, or via the politicians who visit us on their way to the White House.

Perhaps the United States does not really understand us either, if it is even possible to talk of the United States in the singular, as a single entity that can or cannot understand something. It is clear that the easiest story to tell is the kitsch one, like the description of the cab driver who took me from JFK to Washington Square, but I started by explaining how difficult I find it to write for Americans in order to suggest that we should begin from those places where we can see eye to eye, and peer into a new dimension.

I do not want to talk about the differences between the
United States and Israel. Seemingly, nothing is easier. Take,
for example, the cornerstone of American democracy and
its pride and glory, the Constitution, and compare it to
Israeli ethnocracy, which refuses, precisely because it is an
ethnocracy, to bind itself to the Law, to a constitution that
would guarantee equality before the law to all the nation's
citizens (and even the word "nation" doesn't work here,
for the Israeli Hebrew word for "nation"—*umma*—refers
exclusively to Jews). If one takes just that example, there is
seemingly no need to explain further differences.

But that is too easy. After all, Americans, even the most
extreme pro-Israel individuals among them, value their
Constitution above all else; yet they know too that Israel
does not have a constitution and nevertheless identify
"us" with "you," over and over again. Therefore, I prefer
to start with an image familiar to all of us, a Hollywood
image, that of the American male soldier, mainly in World
War Two but also later on, in the other great wars that
the United States produced, first in the world and then in
the movies: Korea, Vietnam, Iraq. What always surprised
me, and I am not sure if you have noticed it, because it
might be part of what constitutes the obvious for you, is
the mature, adult appearance of the onscreen American
soldier, not to mention the commanders, officers,
generals. By contrast, in our fledgling movie industry,

Israeli soldiers are always depicted as young boys, almost adolescent in appearance.

There is thus a difference between Israeli military men as they are depicted in our cultural imaginary and those American military men depicted by Hollywood. Either the Americans are supposed to be the same age as the Israeli soldiers but look older because of cinematic conventions or narrative devices, or they simply are older because they were imagined as older. Both options serve my purpose just as well.

Think of William Wyler's heroes in *The Best Years of Our Life* (1947), or Billy Wilder's heroes in *Stalag 17* (1953), or David Lean's *The Bridge over the River Kwai* (1957) and even films from the 1970s such as *Patton* or *Apocalypse Now,* or the 1980s' *Platoon* etc. Why do these young American men look so much older than Israeli soldiers do in our small film industry? I think they answer to different demands. American cinema is supposed to fill its viewers with national pride, confidence in American courage, determination and virtue (with few exceptions, of course). These soldiers or officers or generals, mostly white, transmit virility, self-confidence, doggedness. We can trust them. We *should* trust them. With such defenders looking after us, we peacefully have a good time in the movie theaters. Even if the films are critical, the heroes are still to be desired as men, trusted as men.

I am not sure whether you are familiar with Israeli war films. The best example would be the 2007 Oscar nominee for best foreign-language movie *Beaufort*, where the soldiers are barely men, almost more like pubescent boys. This is true not only in the cinema, but in our culture as a whole.[2] This depiction of the soldier as a shy, naïve, almost confused young boy is a recurring, deliberate theme, just as it is no coincidence that the war is always described as a siege that besets us.

These depictions are not limited to popular culture. Take S. Yizhar's beautiful boys, especially in his thousand-page novel *Days of Ziklag* (1958) about the 1948 war, or Moshe Shamir's heroes in *He Walked through the Fields* (1947), or Shamir's *Alik's Story* (1951). The soldiers are always boyish, not quite yet men, not only in their facial or corporeal representation, but also through the depiction of their inner world, their adolescent emotional problems with Mom and Dad and with their friends, and especially their concerns over how they will appear to the other members in one of the collectives they always belong to. Some have girlfriends, yet even in contemporary novels their pure and asexual lives remain

---

2   One can interpret Ari Folman's 2008 film on the 1980s Lebanon war *Waltz with Bashir* in this context. If it is an exception, it can be so only because it uses a childlike genre, the cartoon. However, its protagonists, who look like cartoon characters, talk like cartoon characters and feel like cartoon characters, appeal to the same imaginary.

unchanged by events, despite the changing attitudes and growing permissiveness of Israeli society over the years.

If I return for a moment to the American male soldier as my point of departure and comparison, I might say that Israeli heroes ask for a different kind of adoration, love and warmth. They arouse, they are supposed to arouse, a desire to protect them, to defend them, hence they are almost always vulnerable. They ask for parental love from the reader and/or viewer, motherly love.

This structure—I would say a solicitation to defend our little soldier boy—has been prevalent in Israeli culture for more than the past sixty years. Within our national fantasy, even though our soldiers protect us, even though in the daily rhetoric they defend us, promise us a safe life, when we read or watch them in fantasy, they are the ones asking for our protection, in return for their sacrifice. The soldier is always portrayed as a son, always in relation to a father or a mother or both, hence his vulnerability, and if you wish—his hagiography.

This is my first proposal for reading our culture from without, using your own culture of images. Is *our* image, as a whole, within American political discourse, that of a vulnerable child? I do not know. Does Israel present itself, in its own propaganda, as a vulnerable child? Absolutely. The most outrageous example so far is a column by a supposed soldier published in a special section ("Appeal to the World") of *Yediot Ahronont*, the most popular newspaper in Israel.

> As Israeli-born and grandson to a Holocaust survivor I am proud to be a soldier in such a moral army. Sitting in a shelter, next to children and elderly people, I call to the citizens of the world: Wake up! If we put up with it, your children will be the next.

Would you guess this was published on January 9, 2009, in the midst of the fire and brimstone Israel was raining on Gaza? Yet the soldier, as a good grandson, is extremely important if we are to understand the Israeli manipulative narrative: we are the grandchildren that the United States and American Jews are often being called on to feel sorry for.

It is no coincidence that the most prevalent myth in modern Hebrew literature—not only in anti-war political literature, but also in the most Zionist of texts—is a Biblical story, the ancient Hebrew Oedipal myth of "the binding of Isaac," which begins (at Genesis 22:2) with the horrible command: "And he said, take now thy son, thine only son Isaac, whom thou lovest, and get thee into the land of Moriah; and offer him there for a burnt offering upon one of the mountains which I will tell thee of."

I can think of a famous drama, Yigal Mossinsohn's *In the Negev Prairies*, that was already being staged during the last phase of the 1948 war, in which the father, Avraham (Abraham), the leader of the besieged kibbutz which is surrounded by the Egyptian army, asks his son to do the impossible, to go out and break through the enemy lines. The father cannot face his own son, so he tells someone else to tell him to go, saying (and I don't even need to look this up, for it has been inscribed in my memory ever since I saw the play on stage some time during my childhood): "Don't tell him Dad orders, tell him Dad is begging." The son dies on this mission.

The extent to which the 1948 war really was a war of the besieged few against the many is a question still debated by historians, but its myth as such remains predominant to this day. And more important for our argument: It is always the son who sacrifices his life for the father. The father remains ambiguous, a sort of victimizing victim.

In 1970 the great playwright Hanoch Levin, in his scandalous satirical review *A Queen of the Bath*, depicted Abraham with his knife raised, standing over his bound son and ready to slaughter him, shouting out at the climactic moment: "I was born to be a victim. I am a victim."[3] That is what the murderous father says to his tied-up son.

---

3   Published in Hanoch Levin, *What Does the Bird Care: Songs, Sketches and Satire*, Tel Aviv, 1987.

However, that particular satire did not change the terms of the discourse. We now have sons who became fathers, and generals who send the soldiers to kill and to die with the same rhetoric of 1948. Politics is a constant crisis in Israel, hence ideology works overtime.

Contrary to what most non-Jews, as well as many secular Jews, assume, the Bible does not play a very prominent role in Jewish liturgy (with the exception of the Book of Psalms). And yet, every day, every Jew who recites the morning prayer reads, after the morning blessings and before putting on his *teffilin* (phylacteries), the story of the binding of Isaac. And if that is not enough, let me also note that the Jewish New Year, Rosh Hashanah, is marked by a two-day holiday, during which one is required to spend many hours praying at synagogue. During these days too, the space given to the Biblical texts is relatively limited. And yet, every year, on the second day of Rosh Hashanah, we read the story of the binding. And what is read on the holiday's first day? The story of Abraham's banishing of his Egyptian handmaid and their son, Ishmael, abandoning them to die of thirst in the desert. In both cases, the common religious denominator, the father, Abraham, is not a strong man, and he dares to commit the most horrible act—to give up his sons. And in both cases there is something bigger and more merciful than him: God. It is the merciful God who saves the boys who have been condemned to die.

So long as there was a God in heaven, one could expect his mercy, and therefore the father could allow himself to be less strong than expected of a father, any father, in a patriarchal culture. Our new, secular culture did not give up on the father, but only on God-as-father-figure. If you will, then, removing God from modern Israeli culture left it even more dependent on merciless father figures and myths of bound sons. This is the key mutation of the Zionist revival, be it religious or secular.

In that secular Israeli culture, the son—not the father—has always been the source of pride. Even when the fathers wrote the literature, and even when the sons grew up and became fathers themselves, they continued to write the myth of the vulnerable son; the son was always the source of hope, of faith, sometimes of arrogance, mainly in the wider sense of seeing the *sabra*, the Israeli-born son, as the culmination of a historical process, as if all of history had waited for two thousand years until the first boys would be born in the Holy Land, speaking a coarse Hebrew, filled with slang.

When Ehud Barak, "the most decorated soldier in the Israeli army," stood in his Israel Defense Forces (IDF) military uniform in Auschwitz, on the fiftieth anniversary of the liberation of the death camp, and said, "If only we had got here on time" (in other words, if we, the Israelis, had saved the Jews) the scene captured well the arrogance to which I am referring.

The literary image of the *sabra* can teach us much about the ideological makeup of the new Jewish society that settled in Palestine, largely because the writers were very faithful, ideologically, to the commitment to build a "New Man." What were the characteristics of this new *sabra*? I have already spoken of the courage and sacrifice. You are familiar with the forwardness and arrogance, known as "Israeli *chutzpah*," which used even to be praised in America (but is indeed prefigured in the image of the Yankee, as developed in early American drama). And I have already hinted at the fact that the *sabra* is described as a victim of circumstances, or a victim of the cruelty of the generation before him, or of the cruelty of Jewish history. In short, he was expected to be cruel, yet his cruelty was forgiven "in advance" for he was the historical answer to the riddle of Jewish history. Look at the events in Gaza in 2009, read the Israeli press during the twenty-two days of massive murderous deployment of twenty-first-century hi-tech weapons, artillery and air power pouring death and destruction over the largest and most overpopulated ghetto in the world, and see how far that particular dream came true—and then became a nightmare.

Another interesting aspect is its external transformation. In Hebrew literature—contrasting with the
Diaspora Jew—the Israeli-born Jew suddenly turned
into a blond. As you delve into Hebrew literature of the
1940s to 1970s, you meet more blue-eyed blonds than
you could meet anywhere else in Israel. Indeed, this trend
was somewhat obstructed with the advance of Israeli
cinema, perhaps because it was hard to find enough blue-
eyed blond actors to fill all the parts.

In the key novel *He Walked through the Fields*, by Moshe
Shamir, one of the magnificent youths is described thus: "If
you were to tear his shirt off his back, near the shoulder,
his white, delicate skin would reveal large sun spots and
golden down." Amos Oz's writing too is filled with young
men whose tans glow with a golden down. As we shall
see, even his high school teacher on the kibbutz, who he
claims slept with him, not only did so very tastefully, to
the sound of Schubert in the background, but she too had
skin flecked with golden down.

And the best example is the classic teenage book series
Hasamba, which accompanied the childhood of virtually
all Israelis up until the 1980s—the story of a bunch of
Tel Aviv children who form a secret group, a children's
military unit of sorts, which fights the British, then
the Arabs, and of course criminals as well. Its revered
commander, a model to us all, Yaron Zehavi, was always

courageous, sensitive, devoted—and very, very fair-haired. This self-representation has hardly changed in over two generations. Hundreds of thousands of Israelis read these books and learn to identify themselves as vulnerable, brave—and part of the Western fantasy that equates a certain, white, type of beauty with justice.

It is also important to remember that the blond hero's Other usually also appears in these books. In Yizhar's works, the "others" are ugly Jews of Middle Eastern descent, or Diaspora Jews from Europe. In Shamir's novel that I spoke of earlier, the Other is a Diaspora Jew, a Holocaust survivor, described as a "podgy bald man," and also as a despicable crook. The fact that these characters were Holocaust survivors did not save them from unsightly descriptions in early Zionist literature. Almost the opposite is true. In our parents' pioneering ideology, those who did not come to Palestine on time were responsible for their own fate. It would take me many pages to describe the shift in that narrative. I can only mention here that sometimes, in a long process of "identification," Israel managed to create a "joint subject": the Holocaust survivor as Israeli hero.

One more point is worth noting. In Israeli cultural studies, the culture written in Hebrew by Jews born in Palestine since the 1930s is referred to as the "native" culture. The *sabra* is the native, and his Other is the immigrant, especially if he came to Palestine after the Second World War, compelled by historic events, rather than choosing to come as a pioneer. But where are these called "natives" in English, or in other languages? Where is the "real native"? Where is "the indigenous culture"? There is no such thing in Hebrew literature, or there appears to be no such thing. In other words, Hebrew expropriated, by the use of the term "native" (*yalid,* pl. *yelidim*), even that status from the Palestinians. Palestinian civilization—for example, the unique embroidery on dresses, the way the fields were cultivated around the houses, the joint guest room for the entire village in poor villages—all this, together with specific features of the spoken, colloquial language, are part of a native civilization, but were never part of our discussion, in Israel, of "native culture." Here, once again, the *sabra* as a kind of creation of a New Man also became the starting point for civilization in our land, allegedly connecting directly back to an ancient civilization, Biblical or Canaanite.

However, a careful reading will show that the *sabra* might be the Western subject of this literature, or culture of images, while his parents—who came from Eastern Europe—are "not-yet-Westerners." The metamorphosis of the Jew from non-Westerner to candidate-as-Westerner is the most central part of Israeli ideology.

The importance of this metamorphosis has been part of Zionist ideology from its onset, sometimes in socialist, even Marxist rhetoric, and sometimes in nationalistic rhetoric. The challenges of this metamorphosis were great. The desire in our literature for a Western physiognomic appearance, which I have described before, can also be seen, for example, in local beauty pageants, where for decades the rare Israeli blondes were always preferred, chosen to represent Israel in beauty contests abroad. The same can be seen in the abundance of blondes in local soap operas and among TV newscasters. While I am writing this preface, the Israeli media, between the Gaza massacres and the formation of a new government, is obsessed with the success in the US of a certain model by the name of Bar Refaeli. I can hardly think of any other normal country where such a success (being featured on the cover of *Sports Illustrated* and being interviewed by David Letterman) would be treated on the news as an issue of national importance. But the news issue is not Refaeli's breasts or the latest scoop in the gossip columns, or even "our success," but rather her image as a "Western chick." How embedded this theme is within popular propaganda was visible in the press during the Gaza massacre. Every day there were photographs of "chicks," most of them blondes, all of them soldiers in the "innocent" army. Is the soldier-girl the new, sexist version of the old, tarnished not-yet-man soldier?

In any case, this Western physiognomical fantasy is an element of something much deeper, namely a desire to differentiate ourselves from our surroundings, here in the heart of the Middle East, to be the exclusive representatives over here of a better, brighter, Western world. When Israeli soccer commentators notice a fistfight breaking out on the field or among fans in the stands, they are always quick to exclaim: "Where are we? In Africa? Is this how we want to become part of Europe?" In another variation, Ehud Barak constantly describes Israel as a "villa in the jungle." Over and over we are told that Israeli violence is necessary, including the killing of innocent civilians, because, after all, "we are not in Europe," as if Europe did not inflict on the world the most horrible violence of modern times, both on the non-Western parts of the globe and on our own relatives, not to speak of the others, in their midst, just over half a century ago. The injunction is incessant: We must be worthy of being part of Europe, of being part of the West. In international math tests, the greatest shame for Israelis is that, in recent years, Iran has scored higher than we have, as if the Iranians are not supposed to excel in math, while we are destined to.

History is always written by the mighty, by the victors. Even if we do not talk openly of bloodshed, of the price of our blood compared to "theirs" in the ongoing equation between sufferings, every discussion about Israel must bear in mind that over 10 million people live in this nation-state and the territories occupied by it. Half of them are

Arabs, but almost 4 million of them live under military occupation, with virtually no law protecting them. Fifty percent of all the prisoners in Israeli prisons and detention centers—in other words, 10,000 people—are "security prisoners," as Israel calls them, in other words Arabs from the occupied territories who are sitting in prison after being convicted by military courts, or detained without any trial at all. Close to 4 million people are currently living under the longest military occupation in modern times, stripped of the right to vote on the laws that have governed their lives for more than four decades.

The Gaza Strip, with its 1.5 million inhabitants, is enclosed by fences, devoid of any independent means of subsistence—it is nothing more than a huge ghetto. The West Bank, with its 2.5 million Palestinians, is sliced up by army bases and Jewish settlements that continue to grow, connected to each other through a network of highways that the Palestinians are not allowed to use. The movement restrictions imposed by Israel include 75 manned checkpoints, approximately 150 mobile checkpoints, some 445 obstacles placed between roads and villages, including concrete cubes, earth ramparts, 88 iron gates and 74 kilometers of fences along main roads. This "roadblock policy" confines the vast majority of West Bank Palestinians to their own village or town. They are not allowed to ride on the same roads that

Israel's citizens ride on, not even in "their own" territory, let alone through "ours."

Usually, the debate turns to the question of what came first. But I wanted to spare the reader this discussion. I just wanted to let these numbers hang: 2.5 million Palestinians in the West Bank, their communities cut off from each other, and on the other hand 250,000 Israeli Jewish settlers, a ten-minute drive away from the State of Israel. That is all. A Palestinian boy born in Tul Karm not only has never seen the Mediterranean, which is just a few miles away, but also has never visited his grandmother, who lives, say, in Ramallah. Forget the reasons. They only lead to legalistic, self-righteous arguments. Take upon yourselves the task of the future historian. What will he, or she, say one day of this apartheid in the West Bank? That it was the "fault of the natives"?

And maybe this is most important of all: a figure from a report published in March 2008 showed that the infant mortality rate among Arab citizens of Israel is double the rate among the Jewish population—8 per 1,000 live births compared with 4 per 1,000 live births.[4] What is

---

4   Israeli Central Bureau of Statistics, "Infant mortality rates, by selected causes, religion and age," *Statistical Abstract of Israel 2007*, Table 3.30, March 4, 2008. www.cbs.gov.il/reader/cw_usr_view_SHTML?ID=580" \t "_blank" _ www.cbs.gov.il/reader/cw_usr_view_SHTML?ID=580_.

the infant mortality rate in the occupied territories? In 2006 it was 25.3 per 1,000 live births.

As Israel increasingly becomes a stronger regional superpower, our cultural need to build ourselves up as a separate, unique, foreign element in the region in which we live only grows. There is something in modern-day Israeli culture that emphasizes more than ever a fantasy for Western homogeneity, side by side with a lack of will—or lack of ability—to cease to live by the sword. Why disarm ourselves if the fences not only help us be safe, but also help us stay in "the West"? Or, in the words of the future historian: Why think of peace, if the price we will have to pay in return is a heterogeneous life? Better to rejoice that our region is becoming a frontier. Why have open borders? On the contrary, we want to close them down. We have an aerial line to the West, over the sea. Have we not thus fulfilled Theodor Herzl's vision?

Israel would not behave the way it did if US political society did not let it have its way. For years what was called the Israeli Left waited for American pressure. It never arrived. Israel is entangled somewhere between its own adventures and American politics. It is caught in a lethal web. The "natural" allies of Israel in the US are those fervent Zionists among the Jewish community. I can hardly find appropriate words for them. I am sure they are willing to see the fighting continue until the last drop of our—both Palestinian and Jewish—blood is spilt, here in a place where they, the US Zionists, could not stand to live.

INTRODUCTION

Israel—despite its claims regarding a hostile world media—is quite a hit in Europe. Not only do Israelis live constantly within the imaginary of the West, but it has become common in the West to see "us" Israelis as part of "them," at least as long as we are here, in the Middle East, a late version of *pieds noirs*.

The identification with "us" works even better with the Holocaust culture, offering the new European, within the context of "the end of history," a better version of his own identity vis-à-vis the colonial past and the "postcolonial" present. Anxious over the masses of Muslim immigrants, legal and illegal, the new European has adopted the new Jew as the convenient Other—progressive, modern, with no beard, no side locks, his wife wearing no "funny" traditional clothes and not covering her hair. Fortunately, these new Jews look nothing like their grandparents.

In short, the presentable Other is quite similar to the European self, who is still relentless when it comes to those others who do not look like him or her, do not dress like him or her, do not conform to his or her values. This is exactly where I wish to intervene, with both a political analysis of the Holocaust culture in Europe (in Chapter 1), and then an analysis of the way Israel won the hearts and minds of public opinion in the West (in Chapter 2), through a special use of tarnished colonial sentiments.

Israel is like a European periphery, where the national ideology interpellates its subjects as the "last outpost" facing "barbaric non-Europe" (for example, Croatia at the threshold of Western Europe faced with Serbia, or Serbia confronting the Muslim world). The criteria for determining what is Western and what is not have always been based on borders of white and/or Western Christianity as the separation wall in the European imagination. But the most famous (and least imaginary) of all the cases is the current objection to Turkey becoming a member of the EU. Even the arguments made by the liberals in favor of accepting Turkey are part of almost the same demarcation ("We should encourage moderate Islam," "The *hijab* is forbidden there by law," etc.). Where is Israel in such an imaginary map? Where are the Jews, after the extermination of European Jewry? (Before that extermination, as we all know, Jews were not part of the West, never accepted as full members of the West, despite the fashionable nostalgia for these dead Jews today). Israel is part of the West, according to this very political definition of Europe. But it is an illusion to believe it possible to draw a line between where Jewish Israel ends and the Arab world begins. (I shall discuss this fantasy in Chapter 4, when dealing with A. B. Yehoshua and his desire to erase his "Sephardic shame").

Some 60 percent of the Jews in Israel are not Ashkenazi (of European origin, Western). Shall we assume that the majority of Jews in Israel are not Western, and therefore an imaginary border might be drawn between Ashkenazi and Mizrahi ("Oriental" in Hebrew) Jews? It would be a mistake, because it would concern skin color, or place of birth, or accent, or cuisine, or certain religious traditions in an almost racial—not to say racist—manner, by accepting a certain "ethnic" difference between Europeans and non-Europeans.[1] My point is that the line between West and non-West, between West and East, does not divide Palestinians and Jews, or Oriental and Ashkenazi Jews, but rather in a very peculiar way it traverses the Jewish people, as a people, or as a nation. We, as a people, or a religion, even those of us who came originally from

---

1   Popular rites and veneration of "saintly rabbis" among Moroccan Jews were much closer to popular Islamic traditions in the Maghreb than to Ashkenazi Jewish traditions.

Western Europe, were never made part of the (Christian) West. And this despite the nationalization that the Jewish people underwent. Even that nationalization did not make us Westerners, I suggest.[2]

A comprehensive analysis of this ambiguity of the Jews as always (and already) non-Western requires in historians and philosophers a profound attempt to historicize Jewish life over the past two hundred years, since the Emancipation of the Jews. This is an ambitious objective and I can only offer here to analyze some political symptoms of this lack of a proper history. All I can say to my readers is that even the standards according to which Western enlightenment defines secularism versus religion as the first maxim of modern societies are strange and inapplicable to Jewish history. Forget our state regulation of matrimonial laws, which are undemocratic and imposed on all of us, cynically blamed on the religious parties (the main victims being women), while in fact they serve the racist interest of the state to prevent "mixed marriages" between Jews and non-Jews (that is, Arabs). But take, instead, such an easy case as that of traditional dietary laws: 60 percent of Jews in Israel observe the rules of *Kashrut*, not only avoiding pork, but

2   Perhaps the hysteria over the "anti-Israeli media," dubbed by politicians as the "new anti-Semitism," in a way reflects the sense of insecurity with regard to still being "outsiders," but that is not my problem here.

also the other restrictions. They do this by choice, not as something that can be explained away by religious coercion. And if that doesn't make my point, take another crucial example: 99.9 percent of us circumcise our newborn sons, and do so on the eighth day after their birth, as mandated by Jewish law. Yet, most of us consider ourselves secular, and this inconsistency cannot be explained by the European standard of the division between the secular and the religious. My point is that even the self-evident division—which Jews accepted as a way of life when they submitted their culture to the European (Christian) imperative to "Be a Jew at home, a human being outdoors"[3]—didn't really grasp the diverse histories of the Jews. Any attempt to gather all these histories under Western history has failed.

It should have been through us that Europe could have redeemed itself for its colonial past. It should have been through us that Europe learned to tolerate Islam, the most prominent refusal to accept Western secularism as a way of life. Tragically, what has happened is the opposite. It is through us that Europe, for reasons I shall discuss throughout the book, intensified its hatred of Islam and the Arabs: our state—presented as the true heir of the Holocaust victims, most of whom looked "very different

3   A famous slogan of the Jewish enlightenment movement, clearly equating being a "human being" with standard Christian behavior and appearance.

from modern Europeans," most of whom were mocked in the same manner that traditional Muslims are mocked today—gave way to the return of the colonial.

If we peel away the belief in the eternity of Zion, an eternity that every nationalist in the world believes about his or her nationhood; if we push aside the ancient religious yearning for Zion, a yearning that never disappeared but was also never acted upon by the believers until political Zionism took over and nationalized the Jewish religion; if we forget the prayers for redemption in Zion, which are still recited daily by religious Jews in Israel, as well as in Paris or Brooklyn or Yemen, we can get at the pure logic of the tragedy: Zionism thought it would politically resolve the exile within Europe—Jews as "Orientals inside the Occident"—not just by an Exodus, by going elsewhere, but by going to the heart of the colonial hinterland of Europe, the East, not to become part of that East but in order to become representatives of the West "over there," far away from the exile we were subjected to "here," inside Europe. This is how Herzl put it, in very crude words, in his programmatic book *The Jewish State*. After his bitter and sincere description of European hatred toward the Jews following the Dreyfus affair, a hatred he saw as incurable, he writes: "For Europe we could consistute part of the wall of defence against Asia: we could serve as an outpost against barbarism. As a neutral state we would remain in contact with all of Europe, which would have to guarantee our existence."[4] This is a symptomatic prophecy, yet the violence it brought about was targeted not only against Palestinians, but also against the Jews from Muslim and Arab countries who were brought to Israel, and against religious Jews who were forcibly "modernized" according to the vision that called for the creation of a new Jew. In short, the colonial border operated both outward and inward. Most Zionists, especially on the Left, and even religious Zionists, accepted that nineteenth-century hatred toward the Jews was the fault of its victims: Jews were "parasites," "non-productive," "non-enlightened," "backward" in other words, not fully human. Something, they all believed, was lacking in the European Jewish traditional way of life. Somehow, this always implied that being normal was being like Westerners. Zionism did not invent this capitulation to the demand "Modernize yourselves!" as a standard of progress. That capitulation found its roots already in eighteenth-century Europe, among the scholars and founders of the Jewish Enlightenment movement. But the Zionist contribution to the "normalization of the Jews" (according to Western standards) was in going to the Orient. The colonized Jews now tried to free

---

4   Theodor Herzl, *The Jewish State*, trans. Harry Zone, New York, 1970, p. 52.

themselves by colonizing others. And this is even more tragic, because that self-distancing from Europe did not solve the "problem." There is not one inner schism within Israeli Jewish society that doesn't look like the return of *that* repressed: modernization, or, better, colonizing the Middle East, did not abolish the schism between "us" and the West.

The huge tension between Ashkenazi and Sephardic Jews—in quotidian life, in neighborhoods, in super-markets, in schoolyards, on the buses, in the hospitals, in many of the political scandals—reflects that unresolved colonized tension. "We" were supposed to modernize "you," who came (or were brought) to redeem yourselves from North Africa, or Yemen or Iraq. "You" were not supposed to remind "us" of where we live, that is, in the Middle East. "You are ruining our fantasy" could be one description of the hatred felt toward Mizrahi Jews in Israel. (The hatred on the part of the Mizrahi Jews toward the Ashkenazi is widely known.) Yet this ethnic tension is not the only one. There is also the tension between the ultra-Orthodox and "secular" camps, a tension that sometimes becomes hateful, almost anti-Semitic in its tone, and for almost the same reasons: "You [the *Haredim*, ultra-Orthodox Jews] are not modern, you are backward, parasites, you are what the anti-Semites said about our fathers."

All this needs to be explained by a certain form of profound identification with an imaginary West, be it Western Europe, or America, or both. All modern Hebrew (secular) culture has been constructed within that imaginary. Even the Holocaust, despite the political role Israel assigns to it by making it part of our national ideology (a role it did not play with such importance between the 1950s and 1970s but developed with full force later on), appears as if it were a "historical accident" (as a major poet once said in a philo-European monologue). In other words, the Holocaust, just like its distant metaphor, Auschwitz, deep in the land of the Slavs, was not a part or culmination of Modern Europe. Here one can see how easy it is to merge the European *unheimliche* past with the Israeli way of seeing/not seeing the Holocaust. (I will discuss some of the European political background of the Shoah culture in Chapter 1.) Of course, the displacement of Hitler, the new "Hitlers," to Baghdad (this terminology was common in Israel prior to the US attack on Iraq in 1991) or to Tehran (right now), or even to the poor in the ghetto of Gaza, is just another silly symptom of our own tragedy of not being able to historicize our life, the *Jewish condition*. I will try to deal with this tension—the center of the Israeli ideological enterprise—in three chapters: on the works of Amos Oz and A. B. Yehoshua, and (more briefly in conclusion) on the great playwright Hanokh

Levin, perhaps the only Israeli-born writer who deeply studied the (comic) aspects of fantasizing about being in the West while living in the East.

The occupation is entering its fifth decade. It ruined Palestine to such a degree that it will take years or generations to be a developed nation-state, if that is still possible. Israel does not really mean to let it become a free nation. Even during the worst months of the second intifada, trucks of merchandise kept going through to sell Israeli products in the occupied territories. It is a huge market for Israel's industry. For decades, Israel has prevented the Palestinians from developing any economy of their own. It took over the control of water resources in the West Bank. It used the Palestinians' labour as long as it needed it. Once the wave of Russian immigration came, it sealed the Palestinians off. And this happened long before the terrorist campaign began. Israel never thought of Palestine as a free nation. Yet any call for a "single state" solution capitulates to the Israeli rejection of an independent Palestine. The vision of "a single state of all its citizens," as some propose, should not replace the recognition that both nations, Israel and Palestine, have a lot in common that divides them deeply, that is the nationalist project. Even if intellectuals and other non-nationalists, on both sides, may find the rejection of nationalism liberating, negation of the deep need for separate national life cannot succeed (on both sides, it has to do with a very new experience, unlike the European one). Besides, any disavowal of national characteristics in the name of the unitary principle may end up conniving with the ongoing discrimination against Palestinians inside Israel. How many of the Israeli university professors who support "a single state of all its citizens" have protested against the lack of Arab faculty members in their own universities? There are so many Arab students in Israel and so few Arab professors, so many unemployed Arab doctors inside Israel. In any case, in the long run the solution will be a bi-national state, in which both nations will be able to run their national lives together, separated by mechanisms that will defend the Palestinians from discrimination and demonization. (Note, for example, how people always talk of independence for the Palestinians and security for Israelis? What about the defence of the Palestinians? What about their insecure lives under Israeli Zionism?)

I hate to turn my autobiography into a political argument. Too many insincere political treatises were written using that trick, assuming that one's life can exemplify a nation (a nineteenth-century innocent novelistic belief). But I shall say that I was born in Palestine, about a month before it became the State of Israel. My home was a Zionist home. Both my parents saw Zionism as their redemption and as a safe haven. Both of them had left Europe in time. My father was a Jewish German militant of the Sozialdemokratische Partei Deutschlands (SPD) who worked in a local factory in his hometown, until a member of his cell, early in 1933, asked him not to come to cell meetings anymore, because it was "inconvenient." I was brought up to despise chauvinism and any form of racism, with the constant comparison of any racism to Nazi Germany. My mother had come to Palestine from Riga, in Lithuania, as a member of the right-wing Zionist Betar movement. Although she quit that organization before I was born, her deep sentimental love for "all Jews, wherever they came from" (in the young State of Israel that always meant love even for Mizrahi Jews), and her extreme sensitivity to anti-religious sentiments— sentiments we all absorbed in the Zionist youth movements in the early 1960s—became part of my own personal heritage. My wife's father was born in Belgium; hiding in a Flemish farm, he lost his own father in Auschwitz. Her mother was born in Morocco. Our language, in which we shout slogans at demonstrations or read about the daily colonial horrors, is Hebrew. Zionism produced us all as members of a nation. However, confronting Zionism as an ideology and practice, I am not only a son to my parents, but also a father to my child. What shall I tell him when he asks me one day about the deepening disaster in

12

the Middle East? What shall I tell him when he asks what kind of lunacy brought us all to be stained with blood? The feet and the fists are Western, I'll have to tell him, but we are the boots and the brass knuckles. And when he asks whose blood it is, I shall answer: I cannot tell, not only because one cannot tell by smell, or density, or color, but because it is both ours and theirs, and there is an awful lot of it.

Before I go on I should thank my friend, the philosopher Oded Schechter, to whom I owe a lot of my doubts and questions; I also wish to thank my good friend Ruth Meisles, and Dr. Alina Korn, who has always been my political guide. My mistakes are mine, but my insights, if there is any value to them, should be credited to them.

1

The Shoah Belongs to Us (Us, the Non-Muslims)

On February 13, 2006, Ilan Halimi, a young Parisian Jew, was found naked and bound, his body covered with torture marks. He died shortly afterward. The police, the media and public opinion unanimously described the murder as anti-Semitic—even though his attackers had not known at the time that Halimi was Jewish. Paris offered the unprecedented spectacle of the entire political spectrum, including the racist extreme right and formerly anti-Semitic conservatives, uniting to organize a joint protest against the outrage. How to explain this unprecedented unanimity? As the *Haaretz* correspondent Daniel Ben-Simon explained to Israeli readers:

> Halimi's murder began as a criminal act but has been recognized as motivated by anti-Semitism.

The entire country has come together in solidarity. Memories of the 1940s, when France collaborated with the Nazis and sent tens of thousands of french Jews to death camps, have come flooding back.[1]

Ben-Simon explained that, for French Jews, "the murder retrospectively justified" "the fear and anxieties that began with the outbreak of the intifada," a period during which they had "asked for protection that rarely came." And, "That is why Chirac attended a memorial service for Halimi at a Paris synagogue . . . There is nothing like a presidential visit to reassure Jews and calm fears." In sum, Ben-Simon could announce to his readers: "Many French Jews have come to feel like stepchildren of the French state. Now they feel as if they are recognized as legitimate offspring."

The journalist went on to recall the desecration of graves in the Jewish cemetery in the French town of Carpentras in 1990:

The Carpentras incident was motivated by Christian anti-Semitism. Halimi's murder is a case of Muslim anti-Semitism. Many Jews see it as the result of a deeply-rooted hatred of Jews that has taken hold of

---

1   France's Jews: No longer stepsons *Haaretz*, February 26, 2006.

France in recent years. No one can convince them otherwise, even though his captors may not have known he was Jewish until after they abducted him.

Writing never proceeds without its slips of the pen. Sometimes it is the author who is revealed in them, but just as often it is something beyond him which speaks through the lapsus to the reader. What is clear from this is, first, that the "new anti-Semitism" is defined not by reference to an analysis of the objective situation, but as how "many Jews see it." Second, unlike traditional anti-Semitism, its perpetrators are ethnically defined. Third, the shadow of the Nazi past, or European experience under Nazi occupation, becomes the present context of that new anti-Semitism; that very past—even if the "new anti-Semites" have nothing to do with that past—is connected to the evocation of "Jewish sensitivity," or, better, to those who can articulate it, whether the leadership of the Jewish organizations or the Israeli embassy. In the week that the media were exclaiming over the huge Parisian march against anti-Semitism, the Mayor of London, Ken Livingstone, was suspended from office for four weeks by a disciplinary tribunal for saying that a (Jewish) journalist was behaving like a concentration camp guard. At around the same time, an Austrian court sentenced the English revisionist historian David Irving to three years in prison for having denied that there were gas chambers at Auschwitz. As the *Haaretz* commentator Gideon Levy wrote, attacking the sentence:

> It is no small irony that it should be Austria— one of the greatest deniers there is—that has sent Irving to jail. For years Austria denied its responsibility in the extermination . . . It sheepishly came back on its positions only after weighing up the enormous political cost this attitude would have. Today, if the country sends Irving to prison so spectacularly, it is of course through application of Austrian law, but it is also to satisfy the international community and Israel, which was pressing for its boycott.[2]

What, then, Levy went on to ask, should we make of the world's silence at the extermination of a million Tutsis in Rwanda, or the 4 million killed in the Congo? "The world does not want to hear this sort of comparison, and if the facts are not explicitly denied, nobody would imagine punishing anyone for this disgusting indifference." My point is that even if Israel benefits from and sometimes nourishes this new "Culture of the Holocaust," it is above

---

2 "Deportation yes, prison, no," *Haaretz*, February 26, 2006.

all an internal European matter, and the Jews or Israel are bit players in that particular drama.

Commemorations

How should we understand this philosemitic offensive, this strident new pro-Israel tendency in Western Europe? These incessant complaints of anti-Semitism, while we can see on television the realities of what Israel is perpetrating in the occupied territories, are one aspect of a culture that has recently appeared in Europe. It involves a very particular reworking of the past. Our history is rearranged by those who tell its story in the present; to understand what is going on here we would need to interrogate not just the vulgarized media expressions of this mode of thinking, but also the work of filmmakers, philosophers and writers. The question is: Why now? Why the contemporary concern with the Jewish genocide, nearly half a century after it took place, compared to its treatment in the period immediately after the Second World War?

Israeli Jews like myself grew up in the 1950s in an atmosphere saturated with chaotic, almost anarchic images of the genocide. They were progressively arranged into fixed form by the dominant ideology: a structured narrative similar in many respects to that which has been created in Europe over the past twenty years. The new vocation of European Shoah culture provokes a certain unease in me, as in other Israelis—whether the suspension of Livingstone, for reasons that have nothing to do with the genocide, or the big march in Paris, or the role the extermination of European Jewry plays in political and cultural Europe. On the upmarket French and German TV channels, Arte or 3Sat; in the big European co-productions—usually between France, Germany and Belgium—for the cinema; in the literature on the Second World War, Auschwitz is everywhere; only Claude Lanzmann could believe that he and his film *Shoah* are the cause of this. It would be facile to see this memorializing culture as a belated crisis of international conscience, or a sense of historical justice that took time to materialize but has now been fully acknowledged; it would be facile also to speak of a new generation's feeling of guilt, without explaining where that guilt is coming from.

The majority of United Nations General Assembly members have emerged from a colonial past: they are the descendants of those who suffered genocides in Africa, Asia or Latin America. There should be no reason for the commemoration of the genocide of the Jews to block out the memory of these millions of Africans or Native Americans killed by the civilized Western invaders of their continents. But there is no international day to mark the extermination of Native Americans or the Slave Trade, no date on which all countries are supposed to recall what the white man did to them, or to listen to the speeches in their honor.

Yet in 2005, sixty years on from its foundation by the victors of the Second World War, the UN General Assembly decided that from 2006 onward, January 27, the date of the liberation of Auschwitz, would be International Holocaust Remembrance Day. Britain and Italy had already established this as their national day of the Shoah, following the lead of Germany, which had chosen January 27 in 1996. The Jewish genocide has since had a universal place in Western culture, as if this narrative had been there from the start. Hollywood had said nothing about the killing of the Jews for many years. The Second World War was treated in bravura form, with successive waves of films on combat, romance, heroism, stories about prisoners and great escapes, episodes from the war in the Pacific (without a word on Hiroshima or Nagasaki, the two leading events in the logic of denial), and, from the 1970s on, comedy series. The break came in 1979 with the Hollywood-produced series *Holocaust*, which largely adopted the aesthetic of the war films. At around the same time, the decision was made to build a Holocaust Museum in Washington D.C.

What had kept the genocide out of sight or on the margins in the decades after the war, when its memory was the prerogative of escaped Jews, anti-Nazis and other victims? As Raul Hilberg has explained, the salvation of the Jews was not a priority for the Soviet Union, Britain or the United States. From 1941 to 1945, their attention was on the war itself, and on the respective spheres of influence they would enjoy once Germany surrendered. The territories behind enemy lines were analyzed first and foremost as sites of production, mobilization and supply: "The all too real decimation of populations under the rule of Germany and its partners was at best a secondary preoccupation." In early 1944 a detailed report from Auschwitz was forwarded by the underground Polish resistance to the Office of Strategic Services, the War Department and the UN War Crimes Commission. In all three cases, the report was buried. According to Hilberg, "The Western Allies did not want their populations to think that they were fighting the war to save Judaism." It was hard enough to explain to an American why we were fighting in Europe. Britain and the US were waging "a carefully controlled war, minimizing their losses and simplifying their public declarations. As a result of this attitude, the liberation of the Jews would be a by-product of victory."[3]

---

3   Raul Hilberg, *Perpetrators, Victims, Bystanders: The Jewish Catastrophe, 1933–45*, New York, 1992, p. 249.

These facts are well known and have been abundantly commented on in Jewish Israeli debates. This is one area where Jewish Israeli approaches and prevailing Western views do not coincide. For the West has avoided—and continues to avoid—the thorny question of how the Allied powers themselves, and above all the United States, treated Jewish refugees before, during and immediately after the Second World War. The glossing over of this aspect of the tragedy has been glossed over in the narrative constructed in recent decades and has resulted in the loss of a concrete dimension of these terrible events, which have been fused into a version that is totally alien to us Israeli Jews. In mainstream Western culture the Jewish genocide takes the form of a story that has always been told in this way. It seems to have come out of nowhere, but the narrative produces a sort of retrospective continuity, as if it had been in place since the event itself. The ruptures and changes in its telling are, generally speaking, ignored. It is the nature of every ideology to emphasize continuity, but what grates here is that the reality of Jewish history has been so distorted in this telling. It has become the narrative of national continuity which begins with the rise of Nazism, continues with the war and terminates in the construction of the memory of the (Jewish) victims.

In Europe, the Shoah has duly become the image of everything that the Europe of today is not: dictatorship, intolerance and hatred of Israel. Thanks to it, modern Europeans know what is their opposite. But why now? Why is it that, in the aftermath of the Nazi defeat, the genocide was only a reference point on which the victors could agree, whereas today it has become the symbol of the Second World War in its entirety—in the cinema, on television, in political clichés, school syllabuses and state celebrations. One answer is that during the unification of Europe, the genocide and the Jews served in the construction of a European identity. The European subject who, at an earlier epoch, had succeeded so well in differentiating himself from the Jew ("he is not like us"), is now eager to demonstrate how much he loves him: first because now "he is like us," and second because he no longer lives here. This is a hypothesis which would have to be verified for every European state.

Displacing Horror

Ironically, Germany has donated the darkest chapter in its history to be the symbol of the new European identity: Holocaust Remembrance Day. It is worth returning to the choice of date, not only because Germany's decision on this has been taken up by the other states, but also because it shows most clearly the process of amnesia through which remembrance constructs itself. Germany did not set a day to remember all Nazi crimes. It did not choose the day of Hitler's accession to power as the date for its official day of commemoration, or the day the anti-Jewish racial laws were passed, or November 9, the day the Nazis chose to unleash what they themselves called *Kristallnacht* and which for years was a non-official commemoration day for many parts of West German civil society—until it was replaced by the new official day. Nor did it choose the day Poland was invaded, signaling the start of the Second World War. Germany does not commemorate May 8 or 9, the date of the fall of the Reich. Why exactly has it chosen January 27, the day of the liberation of Auschwitz?

The German Federal Republic was not, of course, born anew in "Year Zero." As many have pointed out, its judiciary included many magistrates who had served under Hitler. The post-war ban on Nazi Party members working as civil servants was quickly rendered meaningless under American influence. The appointment of Hans Globke—a jurist who had assisted with the Nuremberg Laws and anti-Semitic legislation in the Nazi-occupied territories—as Adenauer's Under Secretary of State and chief of personnel for the West German Chancellery from 1953 to 1963, on the grounds that he was not formally an NSDAP member, was only the most blatant symbol of continuity during those years.[4] The German economic

---

4   During the Eichmann trial, Ben-Gurion ordered the prosecution not to mention Globke's role in the Jewish genocide, in order to accommodate Adenauer.

elite that had provided the material infrastructure for the genocide also remained in place. In the postwar period, soldiers who had deserted the Nazi Wehrmacht received no pension; those who had served in the SS did. In lieu of any official self-examination, the German state has preferred to elide all the questions arising from the Nazi period into that of Auschwitz. No political price would then need to be paid by the Globkes, the Krupps, IG Farben and the SS pensioners; nor would any compensation be paid to those who did resist. Remembered only as the Holocaust, the past now consists solely of victims—the Jewish people— and executioners, the Germans of the past.

This process reached its apotheosis in the aftermath of German reunification. As a stable republic, solidly established within an institutionalized Europe, Germany moved to complete the reconstruction of the past: transforming the memory of Nazism into that of the genocide, and the genocide into remembrance of the Holocaust. Over 8 million Soviet soldiers were killed in the fight against Nazi Germany; some 16 million Soviet citizens are estimated to have died overall during the Second World War, many of them civilians from Ukraine or what is now Belarus. Official remembrance of those deaths seems set to follow the USSR into oblivion; there is scant place for them on Holocaust Day. The same question might be asked of the vast monument to the Jews constructed in the center of Berlin: Would it not count for more if the tens of millions of non-Jews who perished were also honored, in due proportion? Are their deaths of less significance than the others?

Again, why choose Auschwitz in particular; why not Bergen-Belsen, for example, which is at least in Germany? Even if the worst atrocities were concentrated in the former camp, doesn't the choice of site nevertheless repeat what the Nazis' did—relegating the horror to "over there," outside the homeland, far away to the east among the "inferior Slavs?" (The school trips to Poland organized by Israel's Ministry of Education also serve to relegate the Jewish genocide to the margins of Europe; it is harder to imagine these visits taking place in Dachau, Bergen-Belsen or Buchenwald, in the heart of Germany.) Lanzmann's *Shoah* participates in the same distancing process: the horror took place in the east.

Another feature of the new philosemitism is the attempt to forge a German "Judeo-Christian" identity. A few years ago the tabloid *Berliner Zeitung* front-paged a story on September 11, 2004 about a mass Evangelical Christian pray-in at the Brandenberg Gate, with the blue-and-white of Israel's flag prominently displayed across the center of the layout. The German mass media determinedly attach Israeli images in this way as if offering a humanist guarantee of "the other."

What could be more convenient for the representatives of German culture, whether Christian, Liberal, Green or Social Democrat, in the city with one of the highest Muslim populations in Europe—and a country in which racist attacks on them are on the rise—than the symbol of Jewish, that is, Israeli, "Otherness," precisely on the occasion of a Christian gathering? The Israeli flag, like the Berlin streets named after Yitzhak Rabin and Ben Gurion, become symbols through which German identity is thought. The bogus Judeo-Christian tradition does not correspond to any concrete history; it is an ideological invention invoked against Islam, in which the Jew plays the role of the imaginary other.

In Berlin, the culture of philosemitism takes on a particularly frenetic character. A whole array of (Ashkenazi) Jewish folklore is on offer: exhibitions on Orthodox Judaism, performances of klezmer or Hassidic music and dance. In this respect, the Germans differ from other Europeans, but only in degree; in a large part of Western Europe, the violence directed toward the Other hides itself behind this need for an Other who is like us. This is another effect of the reduction of the Nazi experience to remembrance of the Jewish genocide: this newly constructed past—the Jew as absolute victim— serves as a cover for a new Islamophobia that cannot but recall attitudes that Europe once had toward the

Jews: Muslims must modernize, they must become "like everyone else," in other words, like Europeans.

These developments need to be historicized. In the 1970s, young Germans could wear the *keffiyeh* as a mark of solidarity with the Palestinians without being accused of anti-Semitism or revisionism; the Left could pledge its support for the Palestinians—unlike its heirs, the Greens, who are always the first to speak up in favor of Israel. What is more, in Western European countries where there is no real reason for any feelings of guilt, the Jewish genocide plays a similar role, and encourages the development of a sense of guilt in relation to Israel, represented as the homeland of genocide survivors, just as it does in Germany.

Mussolini's Shadow

An example from Italy: defending his decision to send troops to support the Anglo-American invasion of Iraq in the context of massive domestic opposition, Berlusconi made a moral distinction between Mussolini and Saddam—the former, he explained, was not a murderer. Unsurprisingly this created a scandal and the prime minister hastily had to apologize for his blunder. To whom did he do so? Italy's Jewish community—and not without good reason: It was Mussolini who passed the anti-Semitic discrimination laws and under his rule that the Jews were killed for their ethnic origins. But Berlusconi's apology said much about the memory wars that are being played out in Italian political and cultural circles. In a single political gesture, the fact that tens of thousands had been imprisoned, tortured or killed for having fought against fascism was swept aside. Berlusconi had nothing to say about the horrors of the Salo Republic or the invasion of Ethiopia and the use of poison gas against its population. With the collapse of the postwar order at the beginning of the 1990s, the old way of remembering these events is no longer operational. Instead, the conflicts of the past are covered up by recourse to the memory of the Jewish genocide. Again, this is a new culture, flourishing in a country which, in contrast to Germany, had never repressed the memory of the Second World War or the extermination of the Jews. This is why it is simpler in Italy than elsewhere to trace how "Holocaust Remembrance" has eclipsed the living memory of the past.

In 1945, the young Italian cinema announced its presence with Rossellini's *Rome, Open City*; in the 1970s, Visconti's *The Damned*, Cavani's *The Night Porter* and Pasolini's *Pigsty* and *Salò, or the 120 Days of Sodom* all dealt uncompromisingly with the fascist period; Jewish writers like Giorgio Bassani and Primo Levi described the realities of the Shoah. There were no "psychological problems" about expressing support for the Palestinians on the part of either the Catholic Church, which maintained a wide network in the Arab countries, or the Italian Communist Party (PCI), which supported the Palestinian cause against the Israeli occupation, or the broader Italian Left, which has never had an anti-Semitic culture. Yet Italy—both Berlusconi and his neo-fascist allies, and the former PCI—not only turned pro-Israel at the beginning of the 1990s, but has abandoned its basic understanding of the Second World War in order to reduce the whole experience to the Holocaust. Gianfranco Fini, the far-right leader (who regarded himself as an heir to Mussolini), has excellent relations with the Israeli government.

With the fall of Communism, the unification of Europe and the transformation of its economies, the existing friend–enemy structure was swept away. Up to 1989, each side had an opponent against which to unite: for the right, communist totalitarianism; for the left, capitalist exploitation. In the new moral universe of the "end of history," there was one abomination—the Jewish genocide—that all could unite to condemn; equally important, it was now firmly in the past. For the new Europe, the commemoration of the Jewish genocide would serve both to sacralize the new Europe's liberal-humanist tolerance of "the Other (who is like us)" and to redefine "the Other (who is different from us)" in terms of Muslim fundamentalism.

Ideology of Exclusion

Speaking of the social explosions in the French *banlieues* in the autumn of 2005, Alain Finkielkraut explained to *Haaretz* that the riots were directed "against France as the old colonial power, against France as a European country, against France and its Christian or Judeo-Christian tradition." The philosopher went on to complain that France had made too many concessions to the demands of its former colonial subjects. The teaching of colonial history and slavery in French schools concentrated too much on negative aspects, without explaining that the colonial project also brought education and culture, and without stressing the positive role played by Europe and the US in abolishing slavery. Most meretricious of all, according to Finkielkraut, was any suggestion that the Shoah and the slave trade could be put on the same level.

For Finkielkraut, as for the majority of the West's contemporary political leaders and opinion makers, this is where the Jewish genocide plays its part. The Holocaust alone can provide the definition of evil. The great advantage of this is that the Holocaust took place in the past and is now over; we can congratulate ourselves on having awoken from a nightmare. But the other evils are still lurking there. The universal dimension of the genocide is projected to overshadow the victims of colonialism and slavery, who have received

THE SHOAH BELONGS TO US

no compensation remotely comparable to the sums paid
to the Israeli state, nor even had the fortune of being
recognized, precisely because they are still living in
devastated countries or miserable neighborhoods, under
occupation or oppression; situations which have never
ceased to exist but whose moral claims must be rejected.
As Finkielkraut told *Haaretz* readers:

> The generous notion of the struggle against racism
> has been terribly transformed, into a false ideology.
> Anti-racism will be to the 21st century what
> Communism was to the 20th: a source of violence.
> It is in the name of the fight against racism that Jews
> are attacked today: the Separation Wall and Zionism
> are portrayed as racism. This is what is going on in
> France—we ought to be very wary of the ideology
> of anti-racism.

These words came as a shock to some, not least in Israel;
but those who have read Finkielkraut's 2003 essay, "In
the Name of the Other: Reflections on the Coming Anti-
Semitism," should not be surprised. Here he explains
that:

> With time, the memory of Auschwitz has not faded
> but, on the contrary, been enriched [*incrusté*]. The

event which bears its name, as François Furet rightly wrote, "has become ever more significant as the negative accompaniment of the democratic conscience and the incarnation of evil which leads to its negation."[5]

Finkielkraut duly differentiates between the Western democracies and their Holocaust remembrance, on the one hand, and the "continuers of Auschwitz," the non-democratic regimes, on the other. Democratic man, he goes on—"the man of the Rights of Man"—is "man as such," considered in abstraction from his social, national or racial origins. It is for this reason that America "felt authorized to build a Holocaust Museum in the heart of its capital, and to make this museum a national reference point." Within the new narrative thus formed, the Jews and their history constitute the unique test for human freedom; the democracies of both Europe and America "recharge their common principles in the commemoration of the Shoah."

On this basis, it becomes possible to level the charge of anti-Semitism against anyone who criticizes the US or Israel for the treatment of the Palestinian people. This is not really about perpetuating the memory of the genocide but about consolidating a new ideology of exclusion.

---

5 Finkielkraut, *Au nom de l'Autre*, Paris, 2003, p. 15. Author's translation.

Now it is the Jews who are the insiders. What our leaders asked for, it seems, was not the Rights of Man, but the right to belong to the elite. We can now participate in violating the rights of others.

2

The right of Return (of the Colonial): On the Role of the "Peace Camp" and its French Sponsors

Relations with the Public

Never look down on intellectuals. They can evoke the (irrelevant) past when the present is under scrutiny, they can compete with the most horrible injustice by talking about justice, they can use the genocide of European Jews—insisting on its Hebrew name *Shoah*—even when the destruction of Palestinian national life is being carried out before our eyes. Not all intellectuals are able to do this, and it is not just for reasons of integrity, or humility, but also because of factors related to public relations— in other words what becomes, through the media, the "public"—and the intellectuals' relations with it. Nothing would have helped Israel to present what it did to Lebanon (and to its own people) during the summer of 2006, after two soldiers were abducted from Israeli territory, as just, had words such as "justice" not been swarming out of such intellectuals' mouths. This is how the Israeli occupation of the very last remaining Palestinian territories became part of an alleged "Justice versus Justice" debate (Amos Oz: "in other words a conflict between two causes where both are as just, one as the other"). The longest-lasting occupation since the Second World War, subjected to no rule of law but the law of the mighty, slicing the occupied territories into ghettos where soldiers can do almost anything, anywhere, any time—nothing would have made it possible to turn all this into an issue of "Justice versus Justice," had it not been for these intellectuals in the service of power.

Was the filmmaker Claude Lanzmann lying when he wrote this in *Le Monde*, on March 7, 2001, about the Palestinians?

> They have autonomous territories, an armed police force, weapons are everywhere; behind the rock throwers—the young boys on the front line—there are the masked and equipped Tanzim of Fatah. [1]

I am not sure, because I do not know what he really knew. He tried to depict something which did not correspond

---

1   Claude Lanzmann, "Israël, Palestine: la séparation illusoire," *Le Monde*, February 7, 2001. Author's translation.

to anything but rhetoric. Where did that representation ("They have autonomous territories, an armed police force") come from? From Israeli propaganda. In fact, a few months before, the novelist A. B. Yehoshua had described the Palestinian good life in exactly the same way, as we shall see. But my point is not the lies, or the chauvinism, or the lack of human compassion, or intellectual integrity. What I want to underline is the very reproduction of something that seems "obvious"—with the help of a certain type of intellectual. The Palestinians were armed. Yes, that is not a lie. While I am writing these lines, they are still armed ("an armed police force"). But armed with what? With F16s? With tanks? With batteries of cannons? With helicopters? With infra-red screens on their helmets? With electronic devices? No, they have none of those. But here is the key point: "They have autonomous territories, an armed police force." Dear reader, do not look down on intellectuals. Their words have an aura of Truth, and their truth is made of words, and these words are cheap, very cheap: "behind the rock throwers—the young boys on the front line." Those children, who were born under the occupation, living in fear, with memories of soldiers breaking into their houses at night, with memories of fathers—also born during that forty-year-old occupation—being made to strip at the roadblock, memories of mothers screaming with fear, babies who never saw anything but armored trucks near home—yet "They have autonomous territories." Do not look down on intellectuals. They have the power to construct a Truth.

So, when Lanzmann, the expert on memory who, indeed, claims a monopoly on memory, talks with such arrogance (how many Frenchmen experienced such an occupation during the Second World War? And for how long?), one has to ask what was not said, and yet was part of the discourse. What was not said was an idea that has coexisted with Western culture for many years: "They are not human beings." It does not matter what the present justification might happen to be for that maxim: belief in Allah and Muhammad or the fact that "they are all terrorists." They are always suspected of being "too different from us."

Therefore my concern is not a "conspiracy," or lies concocted by intellectuals working on behalf of power, but rather Israel as a state with very good public relations. Yes, we all know it. When we tot up the balance sheet, after all the moaning and whining about "new anti-Semitism" and the anti-Israeli media, Westerners remember the victims of every suicide bombing in Jerusalem or in Tel Aviv, as if they were nice Parisians or New Yorkers, far better than they remember all the horrors seen on TV of the rivers of blood in Palestine, in Iraq, in Lebanon.

Israeli victims— that is, Jewish victims—are never taken for granted, in the manner of Arabs, Africans, or Asians. A Palestinian girl shot in the head by an Israeli soldier remains an unknown victim, while the Israeli girl shot by a Palestinian terrorist is remembered. The same goes for the prisoners: We Israeli Jews all know the names of the handful of Israeli prisoners, as do many people in the West, and, if not their names, at least their tribulations, their tragedy. But the Lebanese and Palestinians who rot in Israeli jails and in detention camps for years are unknown, and are never part of the "problem" unless there is a kidnapping of an Israeli soldier in an attempt to release them. It is not even a matter of memory. You do not have to remember seasonal rains, only a disastrous flood. Their deaths are like rain; our death is the disaster. M. Lanzmann is one of these intellectuals. And he deserves admiration for his talents.

What Do You Remember about Autumn 2000?

There is a simple test to prove my claim: examining what for the West was "obvious" about the start of the intifada in the fall of 2000. What I wish to show is the role played by the Zionist left in cementing the anti-Palestinian public perception so common today. I know it was not only their doing. It is the way of the world. Most people hate losers, detest the weak, identify with the mighty. But they also need, in our "enlightened era," to be just, to have a "secular God" on their side. This is exactly where what is called in France "the Israeli Peace Camp" played such an important role.

I prefer to begin with the role David Grossman played, carefully, almost shyly, yet always willing to obey Israeli interpellations. Here is an article Grossman wrote right at the beginning of the second intifada. This is how Grossman obeyed the call for pro-Israeli writing abroad:

> True, there is no symmetry between the concessions the two sides can make. Israel holds almost all the cards, while the Palestinians have more restricted options. Nevertheless, there is no escaping the sense that Arafat was the less bold, less creative, and more stubborn of the two leaders.[2]

During the same period, Amos Oz was far more aggressive. The meanings he reproduced during those months have since prevailed in the West. Is it thanks to Oz's role in Israeli propaganda, because he was the most diligent writer for the State of Israel? It does not really matter now. Here is what he wrote on October 13, 2000. This would quickly become the official version of the

---

2   David Grossman, *Death as a Way of Life*, New York, 2003, p. 78.

events that led to the intifada, a version which holds firm to this very day.

Ehud Barak stretched this volatile new tide in Israel to its limits when he offered, in Camp David, to give the Palestinians more than 90% of the West Bank and to recognise a Palestinian state with East Jerusalem as its capital city. He even agreed, with clenched teeth, that the disputed holy places in Jerusalem would go under Muslim custody.

To no avail. Yasser Arafat returned from Camp David back in August calling himself the new Saladin. Palestinian press and media immediately began to beat the drums of a holy war against the Jews, "for the redemption of the holy places."

Mr Arafat is a colossal tragedy for both peoples. He has allowed the newly created Palestinian Authority to sink in corruption, and he has incited his people against Israel and against the Jews. Finally, he has initiated this recent burst of hateful violence, in an attempt to inspire a raging fury all over the Arab and Islamic world to start a jihad, a holy war, against the Jews.

As I listen to the rhetoric of the Palestinian official state and media, and of the Arafatesque intellectuals, I am hardly surprised by the lynching committed in

Ramallah. The Palestinian people are suffocated and poisoned by blind hate.[3]

Note the incitement in those lines. Is it really that different from the Likud offensive against the elected leader of the Palestinians a few months later, when Sharon became prime minister? But, of course, since Oz is a "progressive" he is careful to talk about the natives as if he were a social worker talking about children: it was the father figure, Arafat, who "incited his people against Israel and against the Jews." And not one phrase is offered to corroborate such an accusation, not a single quotation of this alleged "incitement against the Jews."[4]

But Oz's article is better read as an introduction to the humiliation of Arafat's leadership, and to the slow delegitimization of the Palestinian leadership, in other words, the contempt for Palestinian independence. (A political question for you: Who paved the way for Hamas—Arafat or his Israeli enemies? Who produced the dead end known as "no partner for peace"?) Israel's theme, already by the fall of the year 2000, was *to frame*

---

3   "Why Arafat must take the blame," *Guardian*, October 13, 2000.

4   Ehud Barak repeated the accusation even after he for a time quit public life. "Arafat sees himself as a reborn Saladin—the Kurdish Muslim general who defeated the Crusaders in the twelfth century—and Israel as just another, ephemeral Crusader state." ("Camp David and After: An Exchange. An Interview with Ehud Barak," *New York Review of Books*, vol. 49, no. 10, June 13, 2002.)

Arafat. Read A. B. Yehoshua:

> We sat down with Arafat, Barak's offer was generous and then [Arafat] smashed everything to pieces, thinking that only through violence and international pressure could he achieve more. This is the cause of the disappointment. And he made a big mistake, because he was facing Barak, not Sharon or Netanyahu, with a broad consensus to finish the deal.[5]

The Palestinian president was not only the Father of the Palestinian nation, but had also already become an international figure, and it was therefore necessary for Israel to identify the popular uprising with the "old terrorist." Therefore, Oz compared him to Saladin, hoping to appeal to latent colonial (Christian) hatred. It is not a coincidence that Oz was more hateful toward Arafat than anybody else in his camp. There is no other writer of Israeli prose who utilizes the arsenal of colonial stereotypes as much as Amos Oz. (I will return to this later.) Oz's Saladin metaphors had already started in August 2000, while the Israeli army waited for the unrest to begin. Note the agony of the writer sitting in his safe

---

5   "Left in Distress," *Haaretz* magazine, October 20, 2000.

haven, watching the natives, barbaric, poor, in the most populated territory of the world, sealed off already then.

I am sitting in front of the television in the living room, seeing Yasser Arafat receive a triumphant hero's welcome in Gaza, and all this for having said no to peace with Israel. The whole Gaza Strip is covered in flags and slogans proclaiming the "Palestinian Saladin" … My heart breaks.[6]

Forget for a moment the subject of that paragraph, the "I," the writer himself. Leave to one side the *Weltschmerz* he experiences. Forget even the ignorance toward the "historical person of Saladin" (as so beautifully described by Meron Benvenisti in response to Oz's incitement in *Haaretz* back in August 2000),[7] the clinging instead to the anti-Muslim and anti-Arab images, the colonial images used in order to appeal to the old Western colonial sentiments. The authentic dimension of Oz's fervor, apart from his total identification with (General) Ehud Barak, is his deep hatred toward the Palestinian desire and struggle. It was he who, during the 1970s, when Israel refused any negotiations with the Palestinians, dubbed the PLO "one of the darkest movements in history." How was it possible then to turn such a man into a symbol of peace-loving Israel? Only colonial sentiments can explain this.

---

6   Ibid.
7   "The specters of Amos Oz," *Haaretz*, August 3, 2000.

In any case, the hatred toward Arafat intensified, especially inside Israel, during the years preceding his death. Every terrorist action was automatically blamed on him. And during Sharon's reign, this hatred reached an aggressive zenith, when every terrorist attack, that is, every failure of Israel's draconian security measures, was followed by a threat from one cabinet minister or another: "It is about time we liquidated Arafat." The "motive" behind this aggression, toward the elected president of the Palestinians, changed from time to time. Sometimes he was not democratic enough, at other times he did not oppress his opponents with sufficient force, and on yet other occasions he was just too corrupt (as if the corruption rampant among Israel's leadership would ever be a reason not to talk to them).

This strategy preceded even the outbreak of the 2000 intifada. It ran throughout the Oslo years, while the colonization deepened, the number of settlers tripled, lands were expropriated, roads for Jews were paved in the occupied territories, IDF assassination squads were killing Palestinian youths, and Arafat kept promising his people independence, as he was stubborn (foolish? optimistic?) enough to trust unfounded promises he had received regarding the creation of two states west of the Jordan river. But when Camp David failed, regardless of anything else, everyone—writers, ambassadors, senior columnists—were on the same frequency: blame Arafat.

I do not wish to analyze the "Arafat theme" in the Israeli press, only to say that it was directed from above, as part of an orchestrated propaganda campaign. It was part of what Israeli political discourse calls *Hasbara*, which literally means "explanation," but more fundamentally means "successful" propaganda.[8] Israelis are called upon, as good patriots, to "explain" the country's policies to the outside world. Professors who went on sabbaticals abroad were supplied with the "correct answers" to give, and so were Israeli writers. So, the "Arafat theme," as well as later themes, began with a political decision from above, and Amos Oz was simply one of the best hacks in this troupe. Yet, I would like to confront this success of the Israeli media with a totally different set of events. Forget for a moment the books (such as Charles Enderlin's *Le rêve brisé*), the essays (especially the one by Hussein Agha and Robert Malley in the *New York Review of Books* in August 2001[9]). Let us follow the real cracks in Israeli belief in the official version.

---

8   So integral has this term become in internal Israeli debates that the online encyclopedia Wikipedia has dedicated an entry to this phenomenon: "Hasbara (or hasbarah) is a Hebrew noun, literally meaning 'explanation,'" etc.

9   Hussein Agha and Robert Malley "Camp David: The Tragedy of Errors," *New York Review of Books*, vol. 48, no. 13, August 9, 2001.

Enter Major General Malka

One month after the intifada began in late September 2000, Major General Amos Malka, by then number three in the military hierarchy and the head of Israeli military intelligence (a post he was to hold until 2001), asked one of his officers (Major Kuperwasser) how many 5.56 bullets had been fired—from automatic rifles, heavy machine guns—in the Central Command (that is, in the West Bank) during that first month of the intifada. This is what Malka said in an interview, years after the event:

> Kuperwasser got back to me with the number: 850,000 bullets. My figure was 1.3 million bullets in the West Bank and Gaza. This is a strategic figure that says that our soldiers are shooting and shooting and shooting. I asked: "Is this what you intended in your preparations?" and he replied in the negative. I said: "Then the significance is that we are determining the height of the flames."[10]

It was a bullet for every Palestinian child, said one of the officers in that meeting. (This is what the Israeli daily *Maariv* had already revealed seven years ago, when the horrible figures were first leaked to the press, probably

---

10   *Haaretz*, June 11, 2004.

by Malka himself). Is this not the right place to repeat Lanzmann's deceptive description? Yes, indeed, for he was referring in his description exactly to the period Malka was talking about.

> They have autonomous territories, an armed police force, weapons are everywhere, behind the rock throwers—the young boys on the front line—there are the masked and equipped Tanzim of Fatah.

It was the first month of the intifada. The history of colonialism is very familiar with this type of scenario: an attempt by the natives to rise up—yes, bitterly, sometimes violently—meets with a horrible military response, a "tough" response, "let them know who is the master, let them forget the desire for freedom, let them forget what we have inflicted upon them, let them suffer even more." The Israeli Chief of Staff Moshe Ya'alon later dubbed this response as "burning their consciousness." When the intifada broke out, he was deputy chief of staff, already the mastermind behind this strategy, an ally of Ehud Barak. The goal was not only to indefinitely postpone fulfillment of the promise to found a Palestinian state, but also to use the unrest in order to break the Palestinians, to reverse the Oslo "mistakes." A few weeks before Camp David, in July 2000, during the preparations for the Camp David summit, Major General Malka reviewed Arafat's positions for the members of the Israeli cabinet.

I said there was no chance that he would compromise on 90 percent of the territories or even on 93 percent. He is not a real-estate trader, and he is not going to stop midway. Barak said to me: "You are telling me that if I offer him 90 percent, he isn't going to take it? I don't accept your assessment."

I said to him that indeed, there is no chance that he would accept it ... I told them [the cabinet members, all Labour and *Meretz*—*Y.L.*] that the difference between me and them is that they are speaking from hope and I am trying to neutralize my hope and give a professional assessment. But Barak saw himself as able to make his assessments without assessments from Military Intelligence, because he is his own intelligence, and he thought he was smarter. Afterward, it was convenient for him to explain his failure by a distorted description of the reality.[11]

Haaretz's senior political commentator Akiva Eldar, who interviewed Malka, wrote the following:

---

11   Ibid.

Malka insists that even after the peace talks gave way to hostilities, Military Intelligence did not revise its assessments. Neither did the research units at the Shin Bet, the Mossad, the Foreign Ministry and the office of the coordinator of activities in the territories adopt the thesis that the Camp David summit had revealed "the Oslo plot" [by Arafat].[12]

And this is how Amos Oz described the failure of Camp David to Western ears. Note how similar his description of Arafat's "inability" to think or act for peace is to the official line presented by Major General Malka:

Ehud Barak went a very long way towards the Palestinians, even before the beginning of the Camp David summit; longer than any of his predecessors ever dreamt to go; longer than any other Israeli prime minister is likely to go. On the way to Camp David, Barak's proclaimed stance was so dovish that it made him lose his parliamentary majority, his coalition government, even some of his constituency. Nevertheless, while shedding wings and body and tail on the way, he carried on like a flying cockpit, he carried on. Seemingly

12   Ibid.

Yasser Arafat did not go such a long and lonely way towards the Israelis.[13]

Did Oz simply get his facts wrong? Was he misled? It is of little importance. He who sleeps with dogs will wake up with fleas. In January 2007, when Ehud Barak declared he was returning to political life, Akiva Eldar summed up his achievements thus, back in those bad old days:

> He dragged Yasser Arafat into a predictable failure at the Camp David talks. Then, when the talks with the Palestinian delegation in Washington were moving ahead at full steam, Barak allowed Ariel Sharon to take a provocative stroll on the Temple Mount. After the intifada broke out, he refused to meet with Arafat, who sought to lower the flames. Barak also instructed then-IDF chief of staff Shaul Mofaz to enter into direct hostilities with the Palestinian security services headed by Jibril Rajoub, who stood like a wall between IDF soldiers and the Tanzim militias.[14]

And, after all this, Barak, before resigning to enter the business world, handed the right not only the government,

---

13 "Even if Camp David fails, this conflict is on its last legs," *Guardian*, July 25, 2000.

14 "Failure is a guarantee of success," *Haaretz*, January 22, 2007.

but the greatest gift of all: In order to cover up his failure to achieve an agreement with the Palestinians, he claimed credit for his success in proving that "there is no Palestinian partner."[15]

We return again to those who helped furnish the "obvious facts" that lie behind today's desperate situation. Did Oz ever review the part he played in the propaganda campaign? Propagandists do not apologize, unless it is part of the propaganda operation. In any case, he never retracted, never apologized.

Silence is unquotable. I cannot even try and inform you of all the events about which these champions of civil rights kept their mouths shut during that very intifada. Those representatives of the Peace Camp, as they are depicted in the Western press, especially in France, kept their mouths clamped during the great massacres in Rafah and Gaza City, and earlier, during the massacres in Jenin and other towns and villages of Palestine. That silence is unquotable, unless the Western newspapers had bothered to ask them for their response during those massacres. But the press did not ask, because it did not want to know, because the function of these writers—fetishes of progress—was never to be informative, nor to be intellectuals. Is this down to bad writing? Bad journalism?

---

15   "Failure is a guarantee of success," January 22, 2007.

Or caused by paternalistic editors who tolerate awful columns from our little provincial outpost? Perhaps. Yet a proper explanation needs more than a superficial psychological portrait of a handful of editors. What is it that makes up this fetish?

The Messenger of the Colonial—The Neo–New Jew

Is the genocide of European Jewry being used as part of the negation of what is happening to the Palestinians? Who can doubt it? When Eli Wiesel or Claude Lanzmann or any other of the most distinguished bearers of Holocaust memory are recruited to defend Israel, everybody knows they do so on behalf of the Holocaust survivors and victims, namely the State of Israel. Again, this is all part of the blurred lines between Jews and Israelis, the mixed roles they play, all under one title: victims.

"Allow me to tell a brief story, a private one." This is how David Grossman opened one of his European columns, in 1998.

A very dear member of my family, a survivor of the Treblinka death camp, arrived at my wedding with a bandage on her forearm. She was covering her tattooed number so as not to mar the celebration with a memento of the Holocaust.

I understood then, very sharply, how much all of
us here in Israel are always walking on a surface as
thin as that bandage.[16]

Only in this special genre of "Israeli writing in the West"
does one reflect at one's own wedding party on the
fate of the Jewish nation in general and on Treblinka
in particular. This is such a scandalous example of
kitsch that I will refrain from elaborating on it further.
But needless to say, no Israeli newspaper would have
published such nonsense about an aunt with a bandage,
not even if Grossman had submitted it. Yet the Italian
daily *La Repubblica* published this "reflection" on the
occasion of Pope John-Paul the Second's visit to Israel
in 1998. Of course, the conclusion was that what we all
need is peace and forgiveness and so on and so forth.
Who in the "repentant" West would have mentioned that
what the aunt covered in public was then uncovered by
the nephew? No one. This is not a story about a family,
but about politics in Israel, told not by a survivor or
a son of survivors (the so-called "second generation").
This is a story told by an ideologue. In this story, every
Israeli is a member of the "second generation." Israeli
writers within this genre—writers of columns that

---

16   Grossman, *Death as a Way of Life*, pp. 63–4.

address the good conscience of the liberal reader in the West—repeat the same story: We are the survivors, there is no other place for us but in the Middle East, yet we are Westerners like yourselves, we have the same values as you do, we want peace.

A certain Ilan Greilsammer wrote on September 11, 2003, in *Le Monde*—among other defamations of the Israeli left—the following words:

It is enough to be an anti-Zionist, a-Zionist, post-Zionist, or a new historian who describes the massacres perpetrated by the Jews during the war of 1948 to be welcomed everywhere with open arms. It is of no importance that these Israeli anti-Zionists represent an infinitesimally small fraction of the Jewish Israeli population (How many are there in all? Thirty? Sixty? Out of … 5 million?) or that the solutions they propose refer to completely delirious chimeras, those of an Arab Palestinian state which would guarantee the rights of a Jewish minority [*sic*], for their views are now avidly sought well beyond—and here is the novelty—the ranks of groups of the extreme Left. Out go the likes of Zeev Sternhell, Eli Barnavi, Claude Klein, Yirmiyahu Yovel, Amos Oz, A. B. Yehoshua, and David Grossmann although they represent all that is best and most intelligent in the Israeli peace camp.[17]

In today's Israel, it is not that easy to research the atrocities committed by Israeli soldiers in the war of 1948. People have lost their jobs in Israeli universities for less than that. It is not that easy to demonstrate against the war in Lebanon as, according to Greilsammer, only the "anti-Zionist[s], a-Zionist[s], post-Zionist[s], or … new historian[s]" did. What Greilsammer is really driving at is the following: in any other place in the (white) world, a state of all its citizens would be a reasonable democratic and republican solution, a legitimate political idea—but this does not apply to Arabs. If a French non-Jew were to claim this, he would without a doubt be considered a Le Pen supporter. But it is the role of the Jew, within French racism, to articulate such disdain toward the Arabs. This is the return of the colonial.

Of course the Israeli Peace Camp figures do not have the same values as the liberal readers of *Le Monde*, *Libération*, the *Guardian*, or *La Repubblica*. Of course, not one of those readers would publicly demand the kind of constitution those writers support in Israel. And, of course, not one of the European liberal readers of those

---

17 "Tous les périls, plus la trahison perverse," *Le Monde*, November 9, 2003. Author's translation.

Peace Camp Israeli writers would dare support in their own countries religious matrimonial laws of the type we have in Israel, or property laws under which Arabs are prevented from purchasing land, not to mention Israel's laws of citizenship that discriminate against non-Jews. This is exactly the role assigned by racist Europe: to rid Western democracy of its liberal rhetoric. Read Alain Finkielkraut.[18] The poor man talked too much to *Haaretz*. The gap between him and Le Pen is not that great. But this similarity was supposed to remain unspoken, hidden. The hapless Finkielkraut, talking to a Hebrew liberal newspaper, drowned in his own identification with Israel and said out loud what he was meant to have kept to himself. He "felt at home" talking to the Israelis—about the Holocaust and his own history, and about Muslims, and Africans, and Jews, and of course the West, the great defender of tolerance. Tragically enough, all too many Jews have taken up this dirty gauntlet, to express the old racism with a new form of invented history: "the Judeo-Christian tradition," with one common enemy—Islam.[19]

---

18 See "What sort of Frenchmen are they?" *Haaretz*, interview with Alain Finkelkraut, November 17, 2005, and Finkelkraut, "In the Name of the Other," *Azure*, Fall 2004.

19 "They [Arafat and the Palestinians] are products of a culture in which to tell a lie … creates no dissonance. They don't suffer from the problem of telling lies that exists in Judeo-Christian culture. Truth is seen as an irrelevant category. There is only that which serves your purpose and that which doesn't. They see themselves as emissaries of a national movement for whom everything is permissible. There is no

The issue here is not that of Jewish racism, or Jewish hostility toward Arabs or Muslims, not because these do not exist, but because we are dealing here with the Western media. The question here is not Jewish racism per se, but rather *the Western role assigned to Jews vis-à-vis Arabs.* This is the ideological context in which it became self-evidently correct to wash over colonial crimes with slogans of "victims' rights," or "love of peace," or "yearning for peace." The new Jew was once a member of a kibbutz, a good and decent socialist, who, as we all remember, turned the desert green. The neo–new Jew has a completely different role. Either he is an Israeli or pro-Israeli, and he has to remind Europe that the Jews are the bearers of Europe's memory of evil. Our collective memory is the only place to deal with absolute memory, the ultimate story of human suffering. We are not dealing here with a political agenda, nor with a political act. It is rather to do simply with images with which we can identify. This is how Martine Silber opened a long column about Amos Oz:

> When he speaks, he leans towards his interlocutor, as if he were dealing with an adversary, a student, a child. Completely absorbed by what he is saying,

---

such thing as 'the truth.'" ("Camp David and After: An Exchange," *New York Review of Books*).

he demands—by his attitude, his look, his voice, the pauses he makes, as much as by the content of what he says—complete attention. Indefatigable, determined and rigorous, his certainties and his serenity rest on ancient and indelible suffering. We can get a glimpse of these if we refer to a collection of texts published in 1995 by Calmann-Lévy: *Les deux morts de ma grand-mère*. He was born in 1939, in Jerusalem, under the British Mandate. His grandfather had fled Odessa after the October Revolution. Although a Zionist, he had left for Vilnius in Poland. In 1931, exhausted by the anti-Semitic persecution, it was still not towards Zion that he turned: he requested an American passport which was refused to him. He was also refused entry to England and France. He was then "sufficiently mad" to ask for German citizenship. Finally, he settled "on Asia," Zion, Jerusalem. It was not the paradise on earth that he had described in the bad poems he had composed, but rather a primitive, noisy, dusty, agitated city, in which culture was totally absent.[20]

Needless to say, the subject of this interview was the allegedly self-evident aspiration for peace, limited to the

---

20   *Le Monde*, May 7, 2002. Author's translation.

Israeli side, of course. Nor need we be surprised at the use of the timeworn formula of "Justice versus Justice":

It is a conflict between what is just and what is just, between Good and Good, sometimes between evil and evil, but never, *never*, between the Good and the Evil. And everyone knows what the solution will be, everybody knows that one day there will be two states.

But that formula was just as accurate in 1967, in 1977, in 1997, as today. It is a hollow formula, behind which one can easily hide and close one's eyes to concrete injustices, evoking the empty slogan of "Justice versus Justice." With the use of the superficial "Justice versus Justice" theme, one does not have to take sides; one is exempt from taking a real moral stance. If each side is as just as the other, one is fully entitled to stick up for one's own ethnic group.

But, as I have said, this is not about a political agenda. It is about the iconization of politics. Oz or Grossman will tell you about their relatives who survived the Holocaust, as does Finkielkraut. There is no real political or philosophical discourse here, apart from: "We are here to remind you that evil at its worst did take place, and took place against us. The least you can do now is to not identify with the victims of our forty-year-old occupation. You owe us that much at least."

61

Does this discourse spring from the hatred of Arabs and Muslims? Not at all. One did not have to wait for Finkielkraut's scandalous interview in *Haaretz* to sense that. It was in the air all along; it is the return of the colonial. But it is insufficient just to say "they are Jews and that is why they defend Israel's colonial crimes," not only because such talk can easily become anti-Semitic, but because the question has always been the arena in which these pro-Israeli propagandists play. And the best way to examine this is through the discourse on the right of return for Palestinian refugees. Here the theme of colonial anxiety—"they will drown us, these masses of refugees"—was most carefully developed.

Mama, the Arabs Are Coming!

The old Western colonial discourse of mistrust of the Arabs needed the Israeli Peace Camp's intellectuals "to tell the Truth." Credited with personal integrity, Israeli writers depicted the Israeli as the eternal victim of the Palestinians:

> Already in 1967 I was one of the very few Israelis invoking the solution of two neighboring states, with Jerusalem as the capital city of both, reciprocal recognition and mutual acceptance. Since then, for

many years, my own people treated me like a traitor. My children at school suffered all manner of insults, accused of being the children of one ready to sell off his homeland . . . I pause to reflect. I remember how in the old days a single phone booth would have sufficed to contain the entire national assembly of Israeli peace activists. We could literally count ourselves on the tip of our fingers, a tiny minority among minorities. Today everything is different. More than half the nation is with us. . . . Yet the Palestinians said no.[21]

Forget for a moment how Israel turns into the victim through this representation. Note rather how much of the war between narratives is being put upon the shoulders of the "sincerity" of the "honest writer."

The text is, of course, a mixture of truth and fiction. Oz's children grew up in a kibbutz, and if they suffered there it was never because of his political positions back in 1967.[22] Yet in France, as in England or Germany, he is a representative of a nation, and as such he plays a role within the European need for an Other that is part of the *European*, an imaginary that denies the Muslim, the Arab,

---

21 Amos Oz, "The Specters of Saladin," *New York Times*, July 28, 2000.

22 At the same time, A. B. Yehoshua was described in very similar terms on Dutch TV. See "Count the Dead," *Ha'ir*, October 12, 2000.

or, if you wish, the colonial present. There is no better theme via which to examine this than that for which Amos Oz became the principal tribune in the West: the Palestinian right of return as the desire to liquidate Israel, the Jews, to drown them in an Arab flood of refugees. The European fear of waves of Muslim immigrants was fully exploited here. This is Oz, after the collapse of the Camp David talks in August 2000:

> Yet the Palestinians said no. They insist on their "right of return," when we all very well know that around here "right of return" is an Arab euphemism for the liquidation of Israel. Mr. Arafat doesn't insist on merely the right to a Palestinian state, a right I fully support. Now he demands that the Palestinian exiles should return not only to Palestine, but also to Israel, thus upsetting the demographic balance and eventually turning Israel into the 26th Arab country.[23]

Perhaps he did not mean to mislead. Who cares? He was not present at Camp David. He could have written: "I wasn't present at Camp David but I am told by Israeli delegates that Arafat demands that the Palestinian refugees

---

23   Oz, "The Specters of Saladin."

should return not only to Palestine, but also to Israel." But, in fact, he did not need to do so. His statement was accepted as truth merely because a "progressive Israeli" had enunciated it. This was sufficient proof for latent Western colonialism to accept it.

Indeed, this idea became the main theme of Israeli propaganda four months later, in December 2000. The IDF failed to put the riots down despite extreme violence. The promises we were all given that there were plans, well prepared in advance, to teach them a lesson, were now drifting like old newspapers in a pool of blood— now also Jewish blood, spilled in a Palestinian terrorist campaign, which was instigated by Israel's assassination policy of Palestinian leaders (which began in November 2000). Barak was due to lose the election to his old mentor, Ariel Sharon. Suddenly, an intensive campaign against the "Palestinian demand for the right of return" was launched. The Israeli press had been full of critiques of the Palestinian demand for that right, four months before the aforementioned winter in Camp David. On December 14, 2000, I was approached by a nice professor from Peace Now's leadership, who told me plainly: "Now we must all write against the right of return."

And, abroad, it was again Amos Oz, who had already carried the torch of that particular Truth, who contributed his dose of rhetoric on the subject. Let us see some examples of this swift fabrication of a political agenda. Here is Amos Oz in *Le Monde*, on January 9, 2001:

> In Israel, the party of peace should now reconsider its position: for thirty years, we have repeatedly said that peace could not come about while Israel administered another nation. Some even claimed that it is because Israel persisted in administering another nation that peace escaped our grasp. But our government is no longer persisting in this direction ...

The Palestinian nation rejects this peace. Its leaders now openly affirm the right to return of hundreds of thousands of Palestinians who were chased from or fled their homes during the 1948 war, all the while cynically refusing to recognize the fate of hundreds of thousands of Jews who were chased from or fled their homes in Arab countries during the same war.[24]

Then came a trail of articles which all responded to the same interpellation. There was no particularly good reason for A. B. Yehoshua to write a long article for *Libération* in January, when no new political argument had been revealed against the "return," or for David Grossman, at

---

24 "Droit au retour Palestinien = annihilation d'Israël," *Le Monde*, November 1, 2001. Author's translation.

about the same time, to do the same on a Jewish website. (Of course, most of those articles appeared in many languages, as part of the Israeli propaganda campaign.)

It is important to end this discussion with two comments. First, the Palestinians did not raise the issue of the right of return at Camp David. As *Haaretz* revealed some years later:

> In a lecture at Princeton University in March 2002, Prof. Mati Steinberg [until the middle of 2003 a special advisor to the head of Shin Bet] argued that the Camp David summit failed because of the dispute over the Temple Mount—not over the issue of the right of return, *which was barely discussed at that summit and was born retrospectively in Israel in order to create the internal consensus* [my emphasis].[25]

I am not going to discuss the tragedy of a writer who trusted the state apparatus because of his extreme *étatism*, his almost erotic attraction to military generals. I am interested in the march of French fools who followed that Israeli spin of January 2001. Eli Wiesel wrote thus

---

25   More famously, and even earlier, Hussein Agha and Robert Malley remarked: "While insisting on the Palestinian refugees' right to return to homes lost in 1948, they were prepared to tie this right to a mechanism of implementation providing alternative choices for the refugees while limiting the numbers returning to Israel proper" (Agha and Malley, "Camp David: The Tragedy of Errors").

nine days after Amos Oz renewed his campaign against the return:

> The Palestinians are also insisting on the "right to return" of more than 3 million refugees. On this, Israel is united in its refusal. The most fervent pacificists, including the great writers Amos Oz, A. B. Yehoshua and David Grossman, are publicly opposed. And vigorously so. The solution of a massive return is unthinkable. To bring 3 million Palestinians to Israel would mean its physical suicide, which is something that no Israeli of good faith can accept.[26]

Note the importance of the namedropping, of swearing by certain names. This is how the colonial now returns: in the name of the victims. When Eli Wiesel is called to the flag, everything becomes about the annihilation of the Jews. Even Oz was already talking—during the raids of F16 on homes and shacks in Palestine, during curfews and hunger, during the long winter without electricity—about the "liquidation of Israel." Two weeks later, on February 7, 2001, Claude Lanzmann wrote with even greater melodramatic fervor:

---

26 "Jérusalem: il est urgent d'attendre," *Le Monde*, January 18, 2001. Author's translation.

Here too, the bearings have been lost. Amos Oz says, for example (*Le Monde*, January 9): "The return of the refugees is the death of Israel." He adds immediately, it is the meaning of his words, that they will have their state and we will have ours, let us build a wall of separation, a great wall of China—to each his own sovereignty; and if they attack us, then it will mean war. The emblematic newspaper of the Israeli left, *Haaretz*, writes today the same thing. This dream of separation demonstrates well the point at which the situation is tied into a Gordian and passion-filled knot. Without the Israelis, the Arab Palestinians will not be able to live, and the Filipinos called over by Israel from the other end of Asia will not help to appease Palestinian irredentism any more than did Sino-Israeli relations, as the late Rabin thought. All this also is now part of the problem, like the de facto internationalization that the Palestinians have so brilliantly achieved. It remains to be seen whether Israel will one day become a target for NATO, but that's another story: these Jews are even more skilled than the Americans with intelligent weapons.[27]

---

[27]   Lanzmann, "Israël, Palestine: la séparation illusoire." Author's translation.

As you can see, the Holocaust was already on the march in the streets of Paris, whereas in Nablus and Gaza the number of Palestinian victims was rising every day. And the march of pro-Israeli propoganda went on. Here is Arno Klarsfeld, shamelessly, now with no hesitation in repeating the jingle:

The root cause is the refusal of the Arab and Palestinian leaders to accept the State of Israel as a Jewish state. The failure of the negotiations at Camp David and Taba is due to the will of the Palestinians to impose on Israel the right to return for the Palestinian refugees and their descendants.[28]

And then, of course—how could we leave him out?— came Bernard-Henri Lévy:

I would say, like Amos Oz, that the inscription of the right to return at the head of the demands of the PLO is a pure provocation, because this right means no longer one but two Palestinian states: the first here, straightaway, on the restituted territories; the other, later, in Israel itself, when the millions of refugees allowed to return will have

---

28   *Le Monde*, December 5, 2001. Author's translation.

turned the Jewish state into a majority-Palestinian country.[29]

Why was it so easy to spread these particular lies? Why were these representatives of Israel—Oz, Yehoshua, Grossman, Yovel and others—so easily accepted by the French media, using such cheap arguments? The discourse was stuffed with primitive images, nourished by the French racist fear of immigrants. With all those texts vibrating the image of millions of refugees entering Jewish Israel and turning it into an Arab country, the "non-European danger" was already in the air. In fact, it had never really disappeared, only now the old xenophobia had found itself new prophets.

29   "Israël-Palestine: pour une paix sèche," *Le Monde*, June 4, 2002. Author's translation.

3

It Takes a Lot of Darkness and Self-Love to Merge "Us" with "You": Amos Oz's A Tale of Love and Darkness

I look upon Israel as if it were a young girl, after all, I am older than my country. It is not yet ripe, but is gradually ripening. I do not know how much longer she may need. Be that as it may, this country—for better or worse—stands steadier today than it did twenty years ago. More and more people have come to understand what may and what may not be expected, and at what price.[1]

Instead of a Foreword

Going through the "reviews" in the French press of Amos Oz's autobiography, *A Tale of Love and Darkness,*

---

[1] "Der Moment der Wahrheit," *Die Zeit*, interview with Amos Oz, October 28, 2004. Author's translation.

one might get the impression that France is a totalitarian state and that all reviewers have to produce the same articles. Some might say that the publisher Gallimard did an excellent job of public relations for the book and managed to extract from every critic and reviewer the same superlatives, while guaranteeing the total lack of discussion of any literary dimension. Worse than that: the writer was sold as if he himself was the book. I shall quote very little from this treasure trove of mediocrity, yet this is the theme that accompanies the reception of the book: "Behind the trajectory of the writer, born in Jerusalem in 1939, there is the trajectory of a whole people."[2] To give you just one little sociological example relevant to this assessment: the autobiography does not have a single non-Ashkenazi character. How can it be "the trajectory of a whole people" given that our nation is composed of 60 percent non-Ashkenazi Jews? During the period when the interviews and the reviews were being published, the occupation—which was already total, lawless, and more violent than ever—appears only when Oz accuses French intellectuals of being "anti-Israeli." The Palestinians are not mentioned at all. Oz is taken for granted as a man of peace in a way I described in Chapter 2. I am not going to "argue" with the long line of reciters in that chorus

2   *Le Monde des Livres*, February 20, 2004. Author's translation.

line. But the subject of the book is a kind of mirror image: loving Amos Oz is loving oneself. Here is a typical paragraph, which reads like official Israeli propaganda.

> All the Jewish settlements that were captured by the Arabs in the War of Independence, without exception, were razed to the ground, and their Jewish inhabitants were murdered or taken captive or escaped, but the Arab armies did not allow any of the survivors to return after the war. The Arabs implemented a more complete "ethnic cleansing" in the territories they conquered than the Jews did: hundreds of thousands of Arabs fled or were driven out from the territory of the State of Israel in that war, but a hundred thousand remained, whereas there were no Jews at all in the West Bank or the Gaza Strip under Jordanian and Egyptian rule. Not one. The settlements were obliterated, and the synagogues and cemeteries were razed to the ground.[3]

Expert propagandist that he is, Amos Oz well understands how much more powerful "complete 'ethnic cleansing'" is than partial ethnic cleansing. He therefore takes great

---

3   Amos Oz, *A Tale of Love and Darkness*, trans. Nicholas de Lange, New York, 2005, p. 342.

pains to describe minutely the "extermination of the Jewish nation" in the territories behind the "green line," without specifying numbers of villages or victims. It is an absolute we're talking about—a veritable genocide, one after which no trace remains of the annihilated nation. Thus: "*All* the Jewish settlements that were captured by the Arabs in the War of Independence, *without exception*, were razed to the ground, and their Jewish inhabitants were murdered or taken captive or escaped, but the Arab armies did *not* allow *any* of the survivors to return after the war." In the face of this totality, the Jews are seen to have committed something far less genocidal, especially when compared to what the obliterators of their memory did to them: "hundreds of thousands of Arabs fled or were driven out from the territory of the State of Israel in that war, but a hundred thousand remained." The comparison is not over. By way of conclusion, Oz reverts to the same extermination that has already been planted in our brain, with some additional details that serve to echo the Holocaust: "there were no Jews at all in the West Bank or the Gaza Strip under Jordanian and Egyptian rule. Not one. The settlements were obliterated, and the synagogues and cemeteries were razed to the ground." Numbers appear only in the central section of the equation. At both ends—the opening and the conclusion that horrify and flabbergast the reader—there is only unadulterated atrocity. This, of course, is an old trick of salesmanship. Please note—the Palestinians are not mentioned in the equation, only "Arabs"; the result is the semantic parceling up of the Egyptian army (Kfar Darom in the Gaza Strip) and the Arab [Jordanian] Legion (Gush Ezion and the Old City of Jerusalem).

The ruin of the Palestinian people—four hundred of whose villages were laid waste, who were reduced to negligible numbers, racially discriminated against and poverty-stricken minorities in their own cities, and hundred of thousands of whom lost all they possessed, including the chance of human existence—this ongoing destruction, which continued as Oz wrote his book, is turned in the citation above into a not-so-frightful event, the situation of many other peoples being far worse, for example the fate of the Jews in Israel. This is the only time the disaster which affects our life to this day is described in the book. This is all that Oz has to say about events that took place during his lifetime. But it is even more cynical than that. Oz has never employed the term "ethnic cleansing" in relation to the conduct of the Israel Defense Forces (IDF) in 1948. Now he does so only in order to say, if it happened, another ethnic cleansing was perpetrated that was far worse, a "real" ethnic cleansing. He would not have used the phrase at all, had the writing of that particular autobiography addressed only Hebrew readers. No one in Israel, except for a few leftists, ever uses the term "ethnic cleansing" in relation to 1948. The book was written for the European mirror glass.

The book itself, apart from this poisonous paragraph, along with a few others, is a cunning work of flattery of both the Hebrew reader and the reader in the West, with the kind help of translators and editors that saved the Western readers some of the most embarrassing parts of that book, to which we were exposed in the original. History in *A Tale of Love and Darkness* tenaciously rides astride the back of the family of Oz the child. This is how his description of the April 13, 1948 massacre of the Jewish convoy to the Mount of Scopus begins: his father was supposed to form a part of the convoy. Luckily for him, he ran a temperature on the evening before and that saved him. His father's close escape does not save us from an almost bewilderingly detailed description of this of all massacres.

> My father was supposed to go up to Mount Scopus in that very convoy, on April 13, 1948, in which seventy-seven doctors and nurses, professors and students were murdered, many of them burnt alive. He had been instructed by the National Guard, or perhaps by his superiors in the National Library, to go and lock up certain sections of the basement

stores of the Library, since Mount Scopus was cut off from the rest of the city.[4]

But since the book is brimming with writers and intellectuals, it is worth noting that here the "intellectuality" of the Jewish victims of the massacre is underscored: "doctors and nurses, professors and students." However, since this massacre came in the wake of, and probably in retaliation for, the Deir Yassin massacre, Oz strings on the following passage:

Four days after Irgun and Stern Gang forces captured the Arab village of Deir Yassin to the west of Jerusalem and butchered many of its inhabitants, armed Arabs attacked the convoy, which, at half past nine in the morning, was crossing Sheikh Jarrah on its way to Mount Scopus . . . (The Hadassah Hospital served not just the Jewish population but all the inhabitants of Jerusalem.)[5]

Thus: ". . . butchered many of its inhabitants . . . ," that's all, after the previous detailed description: ". . . seventy-seven doctors and nurses, professors and students were murdered, many of them burnt alive." The hospital, by

4   Ibid., p. 367.
5   Ibid.

the way, served the public at large; how inhuman of the Arabs! The description of the massacre of the convoy continues:

> There were two ambulances in the convoy, three buses whose windows had been reinforced with metal plates for fear of snipers, several lorries carrying supplies including medical supplies, and two small cars ... In the heart of the Arab neighborhood, almost at the feet of the villa of the Grand Mufti Haj Amin al-Husseini, the exiled pro-Nazi leader of the Palestinian Arabs, at a distance of a hundred and fifty yards or so from the Silwani Villa, the leading vehicle went over a landmine.[6]

The massacre of the convoy is described in greater detail than we have space here to relate in full. Worthy of note, however, is that all of a sudden the name "Palestinian" replaces "Arab" in the description of the "ethnic cleansing." How does it make its appearance? Precisely in the mode of Israeli propaganda through the ages—from Ben Gurion to Netanyahu—in which the Mufti has played the role of full partner to the extermination, the Mufti who was not even in Jerusalem anymore at the time of

---

6   Ibid.

the massacre.[7] But Oz is not really writing his memoir. The following is the reason for the details. It comes at the very end of the horrifying description:

> Not long after this massacre, the Haganah launched major offensives for the first time all over the country, and threatened to take up arms against the British army if it dared to intervene.[8]

This, in a nutshell, is the 1948 narrative. Deir Yassin is marginal. And then, from the comparison between Jews and Arabs, the causality emerges: *they* started it. Not only it is a false way of presenting the causal sequence of events—the simple fact is that by April 1948 the ethnic cleansing was already in full flow, for it began directly after November 1947—but it shows no sign of any "self-criticism," or reassessment. For years, Israelis learned to pay no attention to Palestinian claims or stories. Oz obeys this injunction to an extent that no one else could get away with, for he represents an "ideal" for his readers.

Unsurprisingly, the critics in Israel were part of the "new consensus" that we witnessed between

---

7 On the manipulative use of the Mufti motif please see the detailed account in Idith Zertal's *Israel's Holocaust and the Politics of Nationhood*, New York, 2005.

8 Oz, *A Tale of Love and Darkness*, p. 368.

October 2000 and July 2006. None of them cited the paragraph on the "ethnic cleansing," none mentioned the reorganization of the 1948 narrative. Unlike the French reviewers, who did not read the whole book, there is no doubt that it was read carefully in Israel, and Professor Dan Laor, a Hebrew literature professor wrote: "the barrier between literature and reality was thinned down, and the structuring of the tale, with its varied elements, created an impression of authenticity." He then compared the book and its merits with Marcel Proust's *A la recherche du temps perdu*.

How is it that to European journalists Oz always appears to be a peace movement activist? Well, aside from Gallimard's success in marketing, the explanation lies in interviews such as the following, published in *Le Monde*:

> The conflict between Israeli Jews and Palestinian Arabs brings together all the elements of a tragedy in the classical sense of the term. Two peoples confront one another, each sure it is in the right. The Palestinians want to regain their land. They have no other country that they can call "home." The Jews claim the same land, and the Israeli Jews have no other country that they can call "home." Here

then are two homeless peoples who claim the same homeland … It's a tragedy.[9]

But where is the tragedy in Oz's description of the conflict? The total ethnic cleansing of the Jews or the slaughtered convoy do not constitute a tragedy but rather a pure melodrama, where the Jews, and Oz himself, of course, are the victims. It is not Racine, nor Corneille. At best it is Pixérécourt. That melodramatic genre is the only arena in which Oz is able to protect the little young woman, Israel. Why does he need that "tragic" analysis? It permits him to avoid any criticism of the Israeli side. It is so easy to evade politics by selling some images, empty words that convey nothing. Take that text Oz wrote for *Liberation*, on August 29, 2005, and see how easy it is not to say anything:

Israel and Palestine, for nearly forty years, are like the jailer and his prisoner, handcuffed one to the other. After so many years, there is almost no difference between them: the jailer is no freer than his prisoner.

Can a real writer be so indifferent to the suffering of human beings? Yes, if your career is being built on selling

---

9   *Le Monde,* October 16, 2004. Author's translation.

your own nation as a tourist package. Or, to be less sharp, Oz doesn't exist without his nationalist collective, and that collective has an *imaginaire*: a family is its protagonist, a very homogenized family to be sure; one may even say a family that is too good to be true.

Wisdom of the Aunt

The narrative past of *A Tale of Love and Darkness* lies somewhere in the nineteenth-century biographical chronicle of the family, and traverses periods of terrible trials and tribulations. The grandparents, very flatteringly described, were extraordinary people, according to the book. Their mode of speaking brings to mind Hebrew translations of Tolstoy and Chekhov. Not one of them is a "morbid" or "demonic" character or anything else out of the arsenal that Oz has often depicted in his narratives. On the other hand, though we constantly hear how erudite they were, and notwithstanding the fact that they lived through the most dramatic eras of our time, none of the family ever has anything of significance to say—a new insight, something we have not heard umpteen times previously. All is subsumed in the kind of banal wisdom you encounter waiting at the doctor's, or for the bus, though name dropping is rife.

The trouble with Trotsky and Lenin and Stalin and their friends, your grandfather thought, is that they tried to reorganise the whole of life, at a stroke, out of books, books by Marx and Engels and other great thinkers like them; they may have known the libraries very well, but they didn't have any idea about life, neither about malice nor about jealousy, envy, *rishes* or gloating at others' misfortunes. Never, never will it be possible to organise life according to a book! Not our *Shulhan Arukh*, not Jesus of Nazareth, and not Marx's *Manifesto*! Never![10]

"They didn't have any idea about life," Amos Oz's aunt tells him and he relates this to his readers. We, all of us—the aunt, the writer and the readers—do have an idea about life, of course. Life does not follow *the book*, but is simply *life*. That's how it is. That's the wisdom.[11] What is bothersome in the deluge of names and the display of intellect via name dropping is the fact that no insight has been drawn regarding "life according to a book." The

---

10   Oz, *A Tale of Love and Darkness*, p. 161.

11   This aunt has already represented the writer as a righteous old man in his novel *The Same Sea*: "He is almost sixty, this narrator ... Since he was a child he has heard, impatiently, time and again from Auntie Sonya, a woman who suffers, that we should be happy with what we have. We should always count our blessings. Now he finds himself at last close to this way of thinking." Amos Oz, *The Same Sea*, trans. Nicholas de Lange, London, 2001, pp. 41–2.

grandfather could have said, for instance, that even Moses imposed upon us a life according to a book (after all, Moses is "our very own" contribution to Western civilization— that is to say, there's good reason to parade him). Or else there might have been some true intellectual in the family, one who had read enough Freud to say that, tragically indeed, civilization itself compels us to live "life according to a book." Moreover, this is the context in which people understand their own lives, which is Oz's quest in this book anyway. And indeed, "life according to a book" is a nightmare, not only for the orthodox followers of Jesus or of the *Shulhan Arukh*, of Marx or Stalin, but even in our own liberal existence. And what of Zionism? Is that a "book" according to which one lives?[12] What about Herzl? Ben Gurion? And the building of a new man, the new Jews, which Oz himself portrays in his novels "according to the book"—what about them? Not an insight on the horizon. And so on, through hundreds of pages over which Oz spills the names of dozens of writers—Homer, Ovid, Shakespeare, Goethe, Mickiewicz, Chekhov, Tolstoy, Dostoyevsky, Turgenev, Gnessin, Bialik, Agnon, Tchernikhowsky, Kafka and more. None of them is

---

12　How blatantly Oz caters to "foreign ears" in the analogy between "their Jesus" and "our Shulhan *Arukh*." How little he know of the first-century revolt against the Pharisees, or about the detailed encodings of Rabbi Joseph Karo in the sixteenth century.

anonymous, none of them is "off the beaten path." Not one of them is an idiosyncratic choice by a reader. In Oz's family no one admired a marginal poet, one already lost to oblivion. None of them loved an unimportant author, suffered from a failure of judgement, had the taste of a different age, or read only the fashionable bestsellers of their youth—Stefan Zweig or Franz Werfel, Arthur Schnitzler or maybe even lesser works. After all, only a few of the books of any given era still stock our shelves today. But no, everything in this book belongs to the movement of History that has brought progress—in a kind of cultural teleology. Dear reader, should you have failed to read these classics, you can now imbibe of them indirectly through the mediation of Amos Oz's aunts and grandmothers. This is the same classic canon as that of yesterday and the day before, for this is an eternal list and the Oz family has thrived under its protective shade. The narcissistic delight, dear reader, is all yours, thanks to the ideal self of the author.[13]

But after the roll call of names of writers that Oz mobilizes in order to present himself to the reader

---

13   So entranced were the petite bourgeoisie by this description that the critic of the *Paris Match*, a representative of this class, described this "intellectual self-portrait" in terms equivalent to an orgasm in prose. See Christine Gomariz, "Amos Oz—Diasporama," *Paris Match,* May 13, 2004. Do not dismiss this because it is *Paris Match*. None of the more "intellectual" publications dared question Oz's description of the self obsessed with "books" as a representation of the nation.

(as an object of love), one is astonished by the fact that nowhere in *A Tale of Love and Darkness* is there a description of anything from any of the books named, or any insight into any of the readers of all those books. So many authors are mentioned, and yet there is no trace of a testimony of anything having been actually read, only the excitement at the ability to attribute the reading of literature to someone. There is not one original, innovative reading, a shadow of an attempt to hold on to a literary memory, an artistic experience. It is as though the man has read literature and nothing meant anything to him at all beside his own life, or trauma. Only in this way can the following narcissistic outburst be interpreted: "So what do all these panting interviewers actually want from Nabokov and me?"[14] Even Agnon, who enjoys the privilege of a personal description because the author had the honor of a conversation with him, and thanks to the fact that he is a more-or-less-famous Nobel Prize winner, enters this pantheon via the ego of Oz, leaving no mark of any significance. A long discussion of Agnon is used for the sole purpose of "interpreting" Oz's own work, after which, in order to escape from any meaningful utterance, Oz mobilizes a grandmother (not an aunt this time) to give vent to some cliché:

---

14   Amos Oz, *Sipur al Ahava vaHoshekh*, Jerusalem, 2000, p. 36. This section is absent from the English version, for at least he (or his translators) were a little embarrassed in Europe by such forms of self-adoration. Author's translation.

For several years I endeavored to free myself from Agnon's shadow. I struggled to distance my writing from his influence, his dense, ornamented, sometimes Philistine language, his measured rhythms, a certain midrashic self-satisfaction, a beat of Yiddish tunes, juicy ripples of Hasidic tales. I had to liberate myself from the influence of his sarcasm and wit, his baroque symbolism, his enigmatic labyrinthine games, his double meanings and his complicated, erudite literary tricks.

Despite all my efforts to free myself from him, what I have learned from Agnon no doubt still resonates in my writing.

What is it, in fact, that I learned from him?

Perhaps this. To cast more than one shadow. Not to pick the raisins from the cake. To rein in and to polish pain. And one other thing, that my grandmother used to say in a sharper way than I have found it expressed by Agnon: "If you have no more tears left to weep, then don't weep. Laugh."[15]

What did the young writer Oz in fact learn from Agnon? "To rein in and to polish pain." You hardly need to cite Agnon in reference to a maxim that could be picked up

---

15   Oz, *A Tale of Love and Darkness*, p. 72.

in any creative writing class. And since Oz has learned nothing from Agnon he cites his grandmother, because when all is said and done—so dictates the popular wisdom that the reader adores so—it is better to laugh than to cry (but where, in all Oz's oeuvre, is there anything funny?). Again, success is teleologized. Oz knew Agnon before the Swedes awarded him the Nobel Prize. Of our almost forgotten Yossef Berdyczewski, on the other hand, who truly influenced him, Oz does not speak. Berdyczewski is barely known even to Hebrew readers, and thus there is no way of really "identifying with him." In fact, not one of his earlier tales and certainly no novel by Oz owes anything to Agnon, either in theme or style. That is why this influence, a sort of crowning of himself as the successor of Agnon, is framed in terms of his grandmother.

Even when Oz essays some original thought, also floating in a sea of important names, his sagacity slips into grandmaternal wisdom: "Gershom Scholem ... was also fascinated and possibly even tormented by the question of life after death."[16] "Fascinated" is very good but "possibly ... tormented" is better, less positive but dramatic sounding. And that is not all:

---

16   Ibid., p. 423.

> The morning the news of his death was broadcast,
> I wrote: Gershom Scholem died in the night. And
> now he knows. Bergman too knows now. So does
> Kafka. So do my mother and father.[17]

Here we go again—important intellectuals are mentioned, ones that the European and certainly the German and French reader would recognize, but we end up with mom and dad. They were avid readers, as has been divulged earlier, but what they share with Kafka and Scholem is certainly not death or even life after death. Nor is anything said, of course, of Jewish beliefs regarding life after death or of Oz's dissent from these. Nothing of any significance is conveyed. The only thing that comes across is that Oz and his parents belong to the club of readers of German, and of course of Israeli readers, whose world is structured around a reciprocated love for the West. This, then, is the main concern of Oz's book—the shaping of the ideal ego, in perpetual oscillation between the delights of narcissism and their virtuous sublimation.

The following is a short example of this smug narcissism. Oz peruses a dedication that his father's uncle, Joseph Klausner, a Zionist historian, wrote to him: "As I stare at this inscription now, more than fifty years later, I wonder

---

17   Ibid.

what he really knew about me, my Uncle Joseph."[18] I will spare the readers some of the embarrassing paragraphs, and will stick to my point, namely narcissism in its political context. Not only do the readers serve as a collective mirror, but they can enjoy themselves by watching this very specular reflection: we are so educated, we are so intellectual, we are so European.

And now for an even more embarrassing sentence:

And since then I have felt good in the company of women ...

There may also be a vague jealousy of female sexuality: a woman is infinitely richer, gentler, more subtle, like the difference between a fiddle and a drum.[19]

Since when exactly did he feel good in the company of women? Since his teacher made love to him, he tells us. Description of the intercourse is too long to cite, but there too Oz hops back and forth between simple narcissism and the ever-so civilized ideal of the self. Note the European odors lingering on the teacher's sheets:

... and so our poetry reading evenings accompanied by strains of Schubert, Grieg, or Brahms on the gramophone faded, and after a couple more times

---

18   Ibid., p. 55.
19   Ibid., p. 500.

they stopped, and her smile settled on me only from a distance when we passed each other, a smile radiating joy, pride and affection, not like a benefactor smiling at someone she has given something to, but more like an artist looking at a painting she has made ...[20]

Despite the sexual swagger regarding the enchanted coupling with his teacher at the kibbutz—her skin was tanned "yellowy-brown" and on her thighs the down was an "almost invisible gold" (is this more *Marie Claire* or soft porn, one may ask?)—sometimes these narcissistic bouts end in a moment of recoil. For example, after the writer describes himself in terms of the caress of his teacher's gaze, a kind of awareness dawns in him that one should not boast in this way. From this emerge all kinds of ironies. The outbursts are then replaced by a studied description of the ideal ego—the Zionist ideal, the State of Israel and Western culture, and their true representatives— father or mother, and, of course, the writer himself and his humility.[21] Thereby we find the figure of the father

---

20 Ibid.

21 An example of the latter is Oz's comparison between his own professorship and the fact that his father never achieved the aspired position. "Sixteen years after my father's death I myself became an outside professor of literature at Ben-Gurion University; a year or two later I was made a full professor, and eventually I was appointed to the Agnon Chair. In time I received generous invitations from both Jerusalem and Tel-Aviv Universities to be a full professor, I, who am neither an expert nor a scholar nor a mover of mountains, who have never had any talent for

enhanced and even more so that of the son humbly nestling against the father figure. With all these the reader may easily identify, especially the Israeli reader. Whoever wishes to address the issue of the immense importance Oz attributes to his parents, without an ounce of self-criticism—after all, in this tradition of memoirs there are precedents—and to personalities he has encountered and known in his youth, should examine the manner in which the collectivity of his readers is offered a sublime being: with the implicit message "We are so wonderful." This is the structure that can help to explain how—through the character of the boy who identifies with his parents—Oz's readership is so readily excited by these figures.

Wisdom of the Grandson

"When I was little," writes Oz, "my ambition was to grow up to be a book. Not a writer."[22] So he also said to a French weekly:

As a child I hoped to become a book when I grew up. Not a writer, a book: men are killed like flies.

research and whose mind always turns cloudy at the sight of a footnote. My father's little finger was more professorial than a dozen 'parachuted in' professors like me." Ibid., p. 128.

22   Oz, *A Tale of Love and Darkness*, p. 23.

Writers too. But a book, even if one destroys it methodically, there will be somewhere a copy of it that will survive on a shelf, at the end of a bookshelf, in some lost library, in Reykjavik, Valladolid or Vancouver. [23]

This sounds very sublime, of course, and again lures the reader into being moved by such an ideal image of the self. However, elsewhere in his memoir, describing "the bad reader," Oz gives vent to his fears (in a chapter that was not translated).

The bad reader is a kind of psychopathic lover, one that falls upon the woman who has fallen into his hands and tears her clothes off, and after she is completely naked goes on to tear off her skin, and then impatiently does away with her flesh, dismembers the skeleton, and only then, when already gnawing at the bones with his brute yellow teeth, is he satiated: that's it, now I'm really inside, I've made it. [24]

And so we come closer to the way Oz should be read (when it is the book that is actually read rather than simply the

---

23   *Livres-Hebdo*, February 13, 2004. Author's translation.
24   Oz, *Sipur al Ahava vaHoshekh*, p. 37. Author's translation.

publisher's press release): it seems that the book Oz wished
to be is in fact the body of a woman, and the "bad reader"
is none other than a rapist torturing that body. Suffice it
to say that—though it is described here in perverted
terms—the fear of the "bad reader" is not disingenuous.
The citation above is no more than a plea for pity, such
as Oz frequently expresses, usually toward defenseless
women, throughout his literary career. In this book he
explains whence this need emanates. Moreover, his fear of
the rapist or his identification with the weak woman is not
only the basis of a raw demagogic patriotism (and all the
harsh rhetoric against left-wing intellectuals is couched in
terms of the defense of a vulnerable female body[25]), but
also, once the "bad reader" is described, the path is cleared
for sympathetic reading on the part of the "good reader,"
namely he who is willing to make love to the book.

> You, the reader, put yourself in Raskolnikov's
> place, in order to feel within you the horror and

---

25   In an interview with Frédéric Joignot, Oz said: "You point your fingers at us,
you demonize us. It's a disaster for us. During the worst period of French colonialism in North Africa, when horrible crimes were committed in the name of France,
we all knew that literature, the tradition of freedom, the great intellectual debates
all continued. No one in Israel, or elsewhere, said 'Let us boycott France.' But today,
I find the media and intellectual treatment of Israel very harsh. We feel as if we are
being rejected outright." (*Le Monde*, October 16, 2004). Such is exactly the role of
the hero of any good melodrama, from Pixérécourt on: to defend the little helpless
girl.

> the desperation and the malignant misery diluted with Napoleonic hubris, and the megalomaniac's visions ... In order to draw an analogy (the conclusion of which will be kept secret) ... between the literary character and your own self.[26]

This passage lays the basis for a sympathetic reading not only of Raskolnikov but also of *A Tale of Love and Darkness*. The reader is told here: You read Dostoyevsky, so "put yourself in Raskolnikov's place." But note here that nowhere in Oz's oeuvre is there a Raskolnikov— that is, such a modernity-inspired murderer—certainly not in this book, but this statement situates the reader as a Dostoyevsky reader, a reader to whom Dostoyevsky has put such an unbearably exacting test. But this is notwithstanding the fact that *A Tale of Love and Darkness*, with its single protagonist who has no ties with anyone in the world, in no way resembles the polyphony of the Russian writer. Oz's manner of presenting the idea of identification with regard to Dostoyevsky's novels reduces the whole literary conception of nineteenth-century literature to the language of Hollywood's popular realism, or paperbacks you read on the bus or train.

---

26 Oz, *Sipur al Ahava vaHoshekh*, p. 39, in a chapter that is missing from the English version. Author's translation.

More to the point, one could interpret it thus: You, the reader, who has never read Dostoyevsky, read me instead. Take Dostoyevsky as an ideal self and come to me and through me into the world that I offer you, in the name of Dostoyevsky.

On the Ideal Ego—The Hebrew language

In a *Livres-Hebdo* article, we find a very popular image Oz has been using for years. The young Oz grew up in Jerusalem, "an old nymphomaniac who squeezes lover after lover to death before shrugging him off her with a yawn."[27] Where does this image of the "old nymphomaniac" come from? It is quite clear: from the ethnically heterogeneous nature of the city. Read closely and you will find that obsessive hatred toward anything which is "impure." Here again, the "return of the colonial" finds an appropriate expression. The following is something Oz said of Modern Hebrew many years ago:

> The New Hebrew is, so to speak, a flirt in heat. One day she is seemingly all yours and completely with you, at your feet, ready for anything, happy for any audacious activity, and all at once you're lying there

27   Oz, *A Tale of Love and Darkness*, p. 27.

behind her, flat on your back and a trifle ridiculous, and she runs off to her new lovers ... She never forgets, not for an instant, the Prophets and the Tannaim, but everywhere she turns she betrays them with every passerby ... and in all her meandering they are viewed from afar, in the background, like the mountains and the sea.[28]

Here, unlike the case of the "old nymphomaniac," we find a seemingly comfortable (metaphor of the) man forgiving the woman "in heat," absolving her lechery. We find Oz again, and most consistently, relating to the Israeli phenomenon in the form of a "girl." We find here the writer exemplifying the most powerful bond of the obsessive structure—the narrator as representative of the Law. In short, instead of a discussion of language, the key point in the paragraph on Hebrew is a metaphor regarding identification with a "father figure." The daughter is a flirt, yet nonetheless we forgive her. Fathers are pure and worthy of our empathy. So what is this Law the writer so happily defends when it comes to the "daughter figure"? The Law is purity, that of a homogeneous nationalist entity. What do we learn from this metaphor of the writer's

---

28   From the Hebrew original of *Tahat Shemei ha-Tkhelet ha-Aza* [*Under this Blazing Light*], 1971, p. 27. This article does not appear in the English version of the same title. Author's translation.

Hebrew? Nothing. Is his Hebrew Biblical or perhaps Tannaite? After all, the two texts are very different. We do not know and can only say that both Hebrews are "pure" from the nationalist point of view, unlike the Talmud for example, or later Jewish Rabbinical writings. So is Oz's Hebrew the language of a lecherous flirt, in other words heterogeneous? It is most striking how hollow the image of Hebrew is. All the Hebrew reader may glean is some sort of reaffirmation of his own language, however it is used, a reaffirmation which claims that New Hebrew "never forgets, not for an instant, the Prophets and the Tannaim." You, readers, possibly you have forgetten the pure sources of your mother tongue, but she—your mother tongue, Hebrew—remembers. How does she remember? Oz offers us no explanation, but simply the notion of a kind of cultural perfume.

These things about Hebrew are as accessible to the Western reader as to the reader of Hebrew, seeing as nothing has actually been said about the language itself, although an exotic image of it has been flaunted. In a 1994 compilation of essays in English, Oz returned to the quarter-century-old metaphor of the "flirt in heat" and reasserted the same "truth of the Tannaim and the Prophets." But now the "lecherous flirt" was replaced by "a character with a questionable past" for fear of slighting Anglo-Saxon feminists. But what Oz has to say about

Hebrew is not important here. The point is the manner in which Oz places himself in the *sphere of the ideal*, a higher plane of identification whence he addresses the readers—speakers and non-speakers of Hebrew alike. Oz presents himself here—precisely in the pattern that recurs throughout *A Tale of Love and Darkness*—as the spokesman for posterity and defender of the vulnerable maiden, namely the State of Israel.

Yet, one has to read into those ideas about purity of language exactly what Oz shares not with the liberal left in the West, but with the reactionary or traditional nationalists. It is not only the anti-Arab sentiments or the fear of immigration that the reader in the West finds it easy to identify with, as I showed in Chapter 2. It is not "just politics," for it is far deeper: namely, the fundamentally intolerant nature of Zionism as a contemporary phenomenon:

> Like any other language, Hebrew has a certain integrity which I'm keen to preserve and protect from modernization. For example, in Hebrew, the verb usually sits at the beginning of a sentence. This reflects a form of cognitive hierarchy. What's more important? Ever since the Bible, actions have taken priority: before we discuss where, why, to what end and to whom you have done something, let's first establish *what* you

actually did. Languages reflect in a very profound way a certain cultural ethos, a system of values. I believe that the Hebraic value system is a good one and I'd like to preserve it. This system is under threat not only of modernization and from foreign languages. Hebrew is like a person with loose morals: it has slept around and been influenced by Aramaic, Arabic, Russian, German, Yiddish, English, Polish and whatnot. And all these influences have the effect of giving it enormous flexibility. One can put the verb almost anywhere in the statement and it would remain good, correct Hebrew, though it could suggest the linguistic background of the speaker. I often write such sentences, in dialogues, which removes the necessity of stating explicitly that a particular person comes from, say, Russia or the Middle East. When I write dialogue, I'm just a bystander and I always try to be a truthful bystander. But when it comes to a description or a philosophical or narrative passage, then I feel responsible for using and preserving the integrity of the Hebrew language because of the values which I believe are inherent in her deeper structure. I often end up feeling like a kind of Don Quixote trying to defend something which no longer exists.[29]

---

29 Amos Oz, *Israel, Palestine and Peace*, New York, 1989, pp. 54–5.

Why is all this talk of the placement of the verb at the head of a sentence given as a specifically Hebrew feature? It is perhaps true of so many other tongues, and in Hebrew, more than anything else, it reflects syntactic chaos (a linguistic jumble which is the result of indecision regarding a uniform version of the language), a chaos that Oz certainly dislikes. Moreover, throughout the years of Oz's writing career, much has been written and debated regarding the question of whether or not modern Hebrew is a Semitic language (as most philologists maintain) or a European one, with a grammar derived from Yiddish and a Semitic vocabulary (Chaim Rosen and Paul Wexler propounded this view, the latter more radically than the former). Oz has no interest in this debate. All he wants to do is peddle an attractive image, at the heart of which is the writer's self-image, defending something feminine, out of empathy with the ideal of the Ancient Fathers. And so he says of himself and his environment:

Spoken languages are all so slim and poor. Most of the people around me use an active vocabulary of a thousand to fifteen hundred words, and this morsel is fettered to grandiloquent structures and the latest in fashionable patterns from overseas ... I hope that little by little literature that is being written will come to enrich the spoken language. After all, the limits of language are limits and what you are unable to express verbally you cannot properly think through either. The chance to express complexity and nuance is the opportunity to enrich life and live it according to a fine and sophisticated rhythm. [30]

But there is really no point in belaboring the issue. Oral languages are no more limited or restricted than literary ones. Some of the most important Hebrew writers did wonderful things by de-mystifying the "ancient" and "eternal" language. A non-erudite discussion of Hebrew can still say something about the Hebrew of literature and of reality.

Image of the Father and the Defense of Europe

One has to read Oz's attacks against intellectuals in Europe. Not only where he "defends" the pure little virgin—the Israeli nation—from these intellectuals, but also where he demonstrates that there is something else which he hates in the "leftist" position, aside from its anti-Zionism. Here, for example, is what the Israeli author has had to say to the elite of Frankfurt in a lecture on

---

30   Amos Oz, *Tahat Shemei ha-Tkhelet ha-Aza*, pp. 27–8. Author's translation.

the occasion of his Goethe Prize award in the summer of 2005:

> Since the days of Job and until recently, Satan, Man and God shared accommodations. The three of them were unanimous in distinguishing between Good and Evil; God commanded to choose the Good, Satan lured to do Evil, but both God and Satan played on the same board, with Man as their play-piece. So simple everything used to be once, absolutely straightforward.[31]

And after this purely Christian introduction to the lost paradise of the religious world comes the almost central issue:

> Somewhere in the nineteenth century, not long after Goethe's demise, a new mode of thought made its way into Western civilization that put Evil to one side and even negated its very existence. This intellectual innovation has come to be known as "the social sciences."[32]

---

31 Amos Oz, *al Midronot Har ha-Ga'ash* [*The Slopes of the Volcano*], Jerusalem, 2006, pp. 67–8, Hebrew.
32 Ibid,. p. 69

From here, Oz goes on to summarize social science:

> In the eyes of this school, uncompromisingly rational,
> optimistic, wonderfully sophisticated—psychology,
> sociology, anthropology and the economic sciences—
> Evil does not exist. And in fact neither does Good.

And thus, so as not to have to say "Karl Marx" out loud,
Oz frog-marches through the lecture theater before
the Frankfurt dignitaries all the founders of the social
sciences, including Weber, Durkheim, Mauss and others.
But in case this crash course on the history of sociology
and determinism did not suffice, here comes the crunch:

> Several of the social sciences of the modern era are in
> fact an extensive endeavor, the first of its kind, to oust
> both Good and Evil from the stage of human vision
> … "society is to blame for everything," or the political
> establishment is culpable, or colonialism, imperialism,
> Zionism, globalization, or what have you.[33]

And so, in a motley of flattery (the grandeur of German
literature through the ages), ignorance and a "be on our
side" form of propaganda, Oz adds:

---

33   Ibid., p. 70.

Today, after the collapse of the totalitarian regimes of Evil, we have developed a tremendous respect for cultures that vary one from the other, for multiculturalism, for pluralism. I know people who would kill on sight whoever is not a pluralist.[34]

Yet again, we are returning to our point of departure. The Father, the guardian of the Law, is not just an obsessive who tracks down all forms of impurity, but he also knows exactly what the Germans like to hear, and not only Germans. A Jew from Israel stands there, in Germany, takes upon himself the right to speak in the name of the survivors, and ridicules multiculturalism. This is the same multiculturalism that in contemporary Germany is trying to protect Muslims from the demand that they "look like us," that is trying to promote Muslims' right to teach and learn in their own tongue within the German educational system, and to build mosques. This is the context into which Oz contributes his adoration of Europe: I, as representative of the survivors, will speak of the past, in return for silence regarding the murky present—the German dream of an all-white Europe. Nor does he stop there:

---

34   Ibid., p. 71.

Again Satan's work is cut out for him. Postmodernism has hired his services, though in this instance his business borders on the kitsch: a small secret gang of "forces of darkness" is forever culpable for all our troubles, beginning with poverty and discrimination and culminating with 9/11 and the Tsunami. Ordinary Man—is always innocent . . . According to the most fashionable discourse, Evil is a corporation. Public institutions are evil.[35]

This is obviously the place finally to settle accounts with Edward Said, in the name of Goethe of course. And, while he's at it, he can attack the "many contemporary Europeans, haunted by guilt and to the point of paying lip service to everything that is far away, to everything that is 'different,' to everything that is absolutely non-European" as well. He does not even see the irony of expressing himself thus, he whose presence in Frankfurt is precisely so linked to the German guilt complex—the prize, the speech, the hope to get to Stockholm by means of the Green notables of *Die Zeit*. Like other deniers of the horrors of colonialism (Fienkelkraut is just a particularly miserable example), Oz suggests, of course, that there

---

35   Ibid., p. 72.

is a misguided sense of guilt—that which is directed at Europe's colonial past—and there is a justified form. Of the latter Oz does not speak, but it is the foil of the former—it is that which places the Jewish Holocaust in the heart of the European ethos.

One might ask oneself whether Oz rehearsed the speech out loud. How would the term "absolutely non-European" sound to German ears? How does it sound in French? Would Le Pen like such an expression? And how did all those bootlickers in the French press react when this theme appeared in the book we are dealing with? I will tell you: the racist colonialism in them probably approved of such a narcissistic idea of the West.

This is how the desire for "European purity" expresses itself when it comes from an Israeli Jew. Here we touch upon the concrete, the real of our life—upon colonialism. The most authentic thing about Amos Oz—if we put aside the fear of women's sexuality, which is simply a pathetic aspect of his clumsy narratives—is the colonial discourse. It is not a conscious response to the bugle call for the sake of an old cause, doomed to extinction. It is a discourse based on the current Zionist experience. In the historical moment in which we are living, Zionism has no source of legitimization except the old colonial discourse. And this is also the ideological project of the Hebrew literature translated for Europeans (as, for example, in *The Liberated Bride* by A. B. Yehoshua): we shall be the ideal border against what is not Europe and we will grant you the stamp of righteousness, of being *kosher*. Even the pork we will make *kosher*.

Back to the Father, "the European"

No left-wing German intellectual has dared to criticize these statements of Oz's publicly. I do not wish to get involved in a long discussion of contemporary German ideology and the place of the Jew within it, so suffice it to say that Oz is being baptized as the "representative of the new Jewish European People," a "graduate of European culture." The character of his father in *A Tale of Love and Darkness* is a clear indication of this dimension of the book.

> The well-known scholars and writers were impressed by Father's acuity and erudition. They knew they could always rely on his extensive knowledge whenever their dictionaries and reference works let them down.[36]

---

36   Oz, *A Tale of Love and Darkness*, p. 414.

Moreover:

> My father was amazingly knowledgeable, an excellent
> student with a prodigious memory, an expert in
> world literature as well as Hebrew literature, who
> was at home in many languages, utterly familiar with
> the Tosefta, the Midrashic literature, the religious
> poetry of the Jews of Spain, as well as Homer, Ovid,
> Babylonian poetry, Shakespeare, Goethe and Adam
> Mickievicz, as hard-working as a honey bee ...[37]

As I said before, Oz's admiration for his father in the
book is indubitable. Notwithstanding insinuations of the
difficulties encountered by the child of such an exacting
father (much less is said of the misery of the mother's
life with a man she did not love), Oz does not have the
courage to truly judge him. Was it indeed only the uncle's
exaggerated integrity that kept his father from attaining
a university faculty post? Was he really a brilliant literary
researcher? Perhaps he was a mediocre one in a generation

---

37   Ibid., p. 127. It is difficult not to be antagonized by Oz's vanity: his knowledge
of German culture is nowhere near as deep as Said's. Where Oz simply relies on a
few Hebrew translations in championing Goethe, Said read the original. Oz can only
scoff at Said, who was an expert in German music, history, literature and literary history even among the German middle class and city politicians, who were themselves
great "experts" on these matters. Oz offers nothing but disdain. After all, he is the
Guest of Honor—Said is dead, and anyway he was Palestinian.

of truly great men of letters? On the other hand, empathy with the father's suffering is evident on many pages, and the story of the pain of this small family, even when told under the strictest self-censorship and in the absence of any narrative courage, especially regarding the mother, permeates much of the book. The pain remains with the reader long after the book has been put aside. The scanty Israeli criticism of *A Tale of Love and Darkness* is perhaps to be attributed to a reluctance to speak ill of a "celebrity" who has laid out in the open his very earliest suffering, after years of beating about the bush.

What interests us here is the manipulative way in which Oz constructs his tale as a version "through the eyes of the West," meaning through the eyes of the Israeli aspiring to be part of the West, by means of an ideal, namely the European Jew epitomizing Europe-ism. The link between the Western reader and the Israeli reader is defined as follows: your fantasy will be "we are your past." In Germany (and sometimes in France) this is part of the embarrassing tide of a Judeophile nostalgia, much deeper than a mere fad. The Jews of Europe prior to the genocide are described as an enormous community of intellectuals, and Oz excels in this direction, as these Jews are all similar to his father and all reassert the superiority of European civilization:

111

So there they were, these over-enthusiastic Europhiles, who could speak so many of Europe's
languages, recite its poetry, who believed in its moral
superiority, appreciated its ballet and opera, cultivated
its heritage, dreamed of its post-national unity and
adored its manners, clothes and fashions, who had
loved it unconditionally and uninhibitedly for decades,
since the beginning of the Jewish Enlightenment, and
had done everything humanly possible *to please it, to
contribute to it in every way and in every domain, to become
part of it, to break through its cool hostility with frantic
courtship, to make friends, to ingratiate themselves, to be
accepted, to be loved* ... [my emphasis].[38]

There seems little need to enter into a detailed lexical analysis
of the verbs in the latter part of this text, which I italicized.
Do they not all describe to perfection Oz's endeavor in his
lectures, in the memoir, in the interviews, in his seemingly
ridiculous quest for the love of the "European Reader"?

European Civilization and Its Victims

The greatest wrong perpetrated in *A Tale of Love and
Darkness* is the denial of the victims' true identity by the

---

38   Oz, *A Tale of Love and Darkness*, pp. 398–9.

narration of an Ideal Ego (*ein Ideal Ich*). The Jewish nation that was murdered in Europe, in whose name Oz extorts empathy from the Germans, was not a nation of "Europhiles." Most of them bore little resemblance to their description in the book or in Oz's interviews in the French press, where the whole identification of Victims = Europhiles receives a grotesque expression. Most of the Jewish victims of the Nazis did not *"speak so many of Europe's languages, recite its poetry, believe in its moral superiority, appreciate its ballet and opera, cultivate its heritage, dream of its post-national unity and adore its manners, clothes and fashions."* This is simply the desecration of the memory of the victims of the Holocaust, most of whom never went to the opera, never read European poetry.

This contradiction is covered up by Israeli nationalism, Oz's own version of it of course, and the Zionism of the Israel-loving Germans or French. The point of contact between Zionism and its supporters in Europe is not religious—it is entirely based upon enthusiasm regarding the new Jew, who has appropriated, among other things, the Holocaust. Only from such a perspective could Oz have told *Die Zeit*, in the same interview in which he compared Israel to an adolescent girl (quoted above):

In adolescence I had a phobia, that as an adult
I might wake up one morning and find myself
speaking Yiddish. Like the fear of graying hair or
the wrinkles of old age.[39]

It takes quite a lot of vulgarity to speak so of Yiddish, the
language of the Jewish people exterminated in Eastern
Europe, to speak in terms of such rejection, usually to
the German press, to speak thus as the representative of
the victims, on behalf of the Hebrew of the "Prophets
and the Tannaim." Oz deals only with the ideal self of
the Israeli reader, and with that of the German reader
of course. But here we should revert to his linguistic
conceptions, to the place where he talks of the oral
language, to where he stands in adoration of the Hebrew
of the Prophets: "spoken languages are all so slim and
poor." The real people, those who never frequented
operas or concerts, those who were deported en masse
to the camps and to their deaths, were not "ideal" in any
sense. They loved their spoken language, their world
which was burnt down; they were real. And Oz cannot
face up to the real.

---

39 "Der Moment der Wahrheit," author's translation.

The Foreign Ears

At the heart of Oz's literary endeavor there is the appeal to the West: (only) we are of your own flesh, though you have rejected us. It is no coincidence that this rationale sounds "feminine." At the center of the rhetoric Oz explains what exonerates us, what justifies us, what renders us blameless that may never have existed, and the version that he offers us is nothing more than a plea for acquittal from Germany, which is always in that context Western Culture:

> Europe has now changed completely, and is full of Europeans from wall to wall. Incidentally, the graffiti in Europe have also changed from wall to wall. When my father was a young man in Vilna, every wall in Europe said, "Jews go home to Palestine." Fifty years later, when he went back to Europe on a visit, the walls all screamed: "Jews get out of Palestine."[40]

Beyond this assertion, the straightforward one which refers not to the Holocaust but to anti-Zionism, and if we abstract from the implied suggestion that anti-Zionism is embodied in chance graffiti somewhere in Europe (weren't there hundreds or thousands of anti-Zionist or

---

40   Oz, *al Midronot Har ha-Ga'ash*, pp. 79–80.

pro-Palestinian slogans that protested the occupation of Lebanon or the West Bank and Gaza?), we find here a rhetorical device that makes an enormous generalization out of a small aleatory detail. This is the Oz method, like a rhetorical bulldozer and without finesse. Beyond all this there is something even more objectionable: the way the Israeli talks as one who talks specifically to the "German," to the Goy as the "son of the anti-Semite." What can be cheaper than the following statements with regard to Lotte Wershner, the mother of Oz's son-in-law, and her sister Margarette, in Frankfurt, while receiving the Goethe Prize, in August of 2005?

> Lotte and her sister Margarette were transferred to Theresienstadt. I wish I could tell you they were both liberated from the camp thanks to peace demonstrators carrying Make Love Not War banners. But in fact no idealistic pacifists liberated them but combatants clad in helmets and armed with machine guns. We, the Israeli peace activists, never forget this lesson, not even as we struggle against our country's handling of the Palestinians, not even as we work towards peace between Israel and Palestine through a compromise one can live with.

Here, again, slowly but surely, an analogy is drawn between the enemies of Jewish existence, the Nazis, and the peace activists of the sixties in Germany, and in the West in general. On the other extreme end of the equation stands the Zionist left—that "supports compromise" but serves in the army. This is an army "in general"—an army that ensures Jewish survival and liberates Jews—whom peace demonstrators did nothing to save from extermination—from Theresienstadt. This is talk for foreign ears, translated into Hebrew, not the other way round. And this procedure recurs throughout the book, as well as in the booklet of essays *On the Slopes of the Volcano*. In the latter the target is no longer camouflaged—it is Germany and Western Europe—but in the memoir it is the Hebrew reader relishing the fact that the West is our Other: the West sees us, hears us, knows us better now, after we told them what their parents did to us, without mentioning, of course, the occupation or the separation wall.

Amos Oz turns to the Europeans and says to them: we are your own flesh and blood; and to the Israelis he says: we are their own flesh and blood. As far as he and his readers—Europeans and Israelis alike—are concerned, the Jews are the mirror. It is enough to peek at the three essays he wrote in *The Slopes of the Volcano* to realize what tender German/Western eyes rest upon Oz, and how well this serves him.

And then there are the books.

> That is to say, there were always books. In almost every
> home we had in Jerusalem German books or Hebrew
> books that had been translated from the German even
> before WWII—Goethe, Schiller, Kleist and Heine,
> Thomas Mann and Erich Maria Remarque.[41]

Once upon a time, there was a Holocaust and an emotional breakdown; then came reconciliation, and then the
return of literature:

> And so, Gunter Grass, Heinrich Boll, Ingeborg
> Bachmann, Uwe Johnson and especially my beloved
> friend Siegfried Lenz, opened the door to Germany
> for me. These writers and a handful of dear personal
> friends in Germany caused me to lift the boycott
> and to open up my mind and after a while—my
> heart too. They reacquainted me with the medicinal
> capacities of literature.[42]

And then, after this piousness of a seemingly personal
story as a means of telling the general narrative, comes
the usual conclusion—having slung dirt at whoever

---

41   Ibid., p. 23.
42   Ibid., p. 80.

sympathizes with the non-European, that is, with the Other always ingratiating, he says:

> To imagine the Other is not a mere aesthetic tool. To visualize the Other is to my mind an important moral dictum.
>
> This and more—to imagine the Other, if you promise to keep the secret, is also a distinctly sublime and refined human pleasure.[43]

And the only question is what Other is Oz capable of visualizing? From the vision of what Other does he derive pleasure?

The Motherland

None of this tells us much about the path Oz would like us to follow—that which leads to his mother's death. The child has grown up, and yet he prefers to recreate the pain of the child and not to talk of the pain of the adult as he recalls the life of the miserable child. Because the thread must pass through Oz's emotional world, and that world is embedded painfully deep in the heart of the confused reader as well. This literary endeavor is a form

---

43 Ibid., p. 80.

of fetishism that expresses above all a fear of the void underlying reality, a fear of undermining what has been achieved. The fear of nullity is a worthy subject, but one which Oz cannot truly address. This is due to his fear of the "bad reader."

Sometimes, in little glimmers, Oz isolates a sort of mysterious feeling of communion. At such moments he uses that affected authoritative voice that we already know to glorify the writing of the ancients, and through it he remembers his parents.

> I can see them standing there, at the end of the world, on the edge of the wilderness, both very tender, like a pair of teddy bears, arm in arm, with the evening breeze of Jerusalem blowing above their heads ... [44]

Sometimes, especially with regard to the figure of his father, the description is not entirely lacking in sophistication, coming as it does against the background of the Revisionist milieu of Jerusalem, which Oz exchanged for other father figures—the Labor Party tradition—so great was his desire to move on from his parental abode.

The whole process of "conversion," however, instead

---

44   Oz, *A Tale of Love and Darkness*, p. 64.

of occupying the center of the memoir, is barely discernible under the enfolding folklore. Instead of allowing his "guilt complex" (expressed only in the melodramatic declaration "I killed my father" when he recounts his change of name from Klausner to Oz) to become the heart of the drama, he defuses it by delving into a comparison between the two groupings, the one he left and the one he joined. In the Kibbutz the great expulsion of the Arabs in 1948 was seen as justified, and there, as among Jerusalem's Nationalists, they talked in favor of ethnic cleansing. Oz is afraid of doubt, of the tragic. So much so indeed that the "conversion" itself—the heart of the drama between himself and his father—is used as the story's comic relief. A three-page scene is devoted to a speech by Menachem Begin in which he talks of "taking up arms" using a verb that for the younger generation of his day meant "getting laid." Even assuming that this all actually happened, the same joke can be found in an earlier book attributed to some other public figure of the day. All that remains of Oz's dramatic turning away from his father and his father's family is a comic event—the child sniggering in a Begin meeting and cutting himself off from the family. The Oedipus complex, so central to the memoir, has been reduced to a bad joke.

Oz refers a few times, along the way, to his mother's

suicide, but he puts off tackling it until near the end of the book. The heart, the core of his pain, is found in the attempt to reconstruct the things he would have said to her had he had the chance. And although this is a melodramatic technique in its most blatant form, it is nevertheless a heart-rending instance:

> If I had been there with her in that room overlooking the back yard in Haya and Tsvi's apartment at that moment, at half past eight or a quarter to nine on that Saturday evening, I would certainly have tried my hardest to explain to her why she mustn't. And if I did not succeed I would have done everything possible to stir her compassion, to make her take pity on her only child. I would have cried and I would have pleaded without any shame and I would have hugged her knees, I might even have pretended to faint or I might have hit and scratched myself till the blood flowed as I had seen her do in moments of despair.[45]

This is how Oz excuses his perpetual appeal to the guilt complex of others and to their pity. It would have been less reprehensible had he not so fused the history of the

---

45 Ibid., p. 537.

establishment of the State of Israel with the martyrdom of the book's victim, his mother—indeed, that of his father and himself too.

> One of the two rooms in Haya and Tsvi Shapiro's ground-floor apartment at 175 Ben Yehuda Street in Tel Aviv was sublet to various senior commanders of the Haganah. In 1948, during the War of Independence, Major General Yigael Yadin, who was head of operations and deputy Chief of Staff of the newly established Israeli army, lived there. Conferences were held there at night, with Israel Galili, Yitzhak Sadeh, Yaakov Dori, leaders of the Haganah, advisers and officers. Three years later, in the same room, my mother took her own life.[46]

The most terrible moment, almost at the very end of the book, is recounted in the same ironic tone, and there it becomes fused with the presence of Germany in our lives:

> My mother ended her life at her sister's apartment in Ben Yehuda Street, Tel Aviv, in the night between Saturday and Sunday, January 6, 1952. There was a

---

46   Ibid., p. 175.

hysterical debate going on in the country at the time about whether or not Israel should demand and accept reparations from Germany on account of property of Jews murdered during the Hitler period.[47]

Were it not political manipulation we were dealing with, embarrassing for the German or Western reader, one could salute this compelling need of the writer, his wish for omnipotence in face of all the impotence— the lost mother as representative of the West. But we can interpret things in an inverse manner. In the face of impotence, Oz has to put up a façade of omnipotence. So he has to parade as a writer who is representative of the Jewish Nation and thus also of the European readership, a shield put up to save Western civilization from the evil dragon of "multiculturalism" and the East in general. Alas, here, the most intimate memory is lost. At the end of a whole story devoted to his parading as an exiled expert on German culture, his mother's suicide, described as occurring on the day when the issue of reparations from Germany was fought out, becomes just another element of the Zionist Revival. The Israeli reader may take pleasure in the distaste of the departed grandmother for the dirty and disease-infested East. He may, at the same time, be

---

47   Ibid., p. 531.

indifferent with regard to the East as it is now, now that we ourselves are Westerners and that everything is fine— between the Europeans and us, that is. Because Oz is one of us and one of them, and the Holocaust, too, belongs to us all—to the entire West.

Pieds Noirs

One could say that all this is part of a literary world market and the tactics for achieving fortune or fame. One could also speak of that market and of the relationship between center and margins. Oz, just like most provincials selling prose to the center, oscillates between using marginality to his advantage and denying any difference between the margins and the center. Yet there is a difference, a deep one, one that does not disappear just because you close your eyes to it.

Israeli culture—as a very problematic segment of existing Judaic cultures—maintains complex relations with Western culture. Even the idea of nationalism attracts Israelis as a way of becoming "normal," that is, becoming "like the West," the model to which we all had to adopt our vision of ourselves. Under the auspices of nationalistic Europe, nationalism has come to be identified with the trinity constituted by territory-language-people.

The situation is even more complicated. Our forefathers adjusted their culture to a foreign model, in a long and tortuous process, with physical extermination as one of its stages, and this dislocation has never been mended. On the contrary—Zionism took it one step further when it promised the Jews that it would be mended through the colonization of another people. As we have noted, Herzl defined the settlement in Asia, at one and the same time, as an escape from anti-Semitism and as a bulwark for the West against the barbarians of Asia.

Conformity with European norms (in dress habits, for example, over the last two centuries) was achieved by accepting an internal contradiction that was never resolved. Western civilization had no need to resolve it in order to "be itself." But the Jews, in order to "be themselves," had to divide themselves between being a Jew ("at home") and being a human (outdoors). As far as the Christian is concerned, no such duality exists, for, in the context of the culture of which we speak, being a man is tantamount to being a (Caucasian) Christian. This is the very heart of European colonialism. Israeli Jews are a very special kind of *colonized colonizers*, a late, perhaps the latest, version of *pieds noirs*. In short: we are part of you as long as we are here. To claim otherwise requires a lot of narcissistic denial, a lot of darkness and a lot of self-love.

"I Don't Even Want to Know Their Names"— On Hatred for the East: A. B. Yehoshua and the Shame of Being Sephardi

Immediately after the outbreak of the Second Lebanon War in July 2006, as the destruction and brutality were reaching a peak, the novelist and essayist A. B. Yehoshua told *Haaretz,* in his characteristically crude way, speaking in Hebrew about the Arabs: "Finally, we've got a just war, so we don't need to gnaw it too much until it becomes unjust."[1] Yehoshua, of course, was no less supportive of the previous wars. In all of them, he regarded Israel as just. He supported the Israeli Defence Forces when the second intifada erupted in 2000 and he backed the IDF when the First Lebanon War began in 1982. So what is at issue is less the fact of his support, and more the brutal style in which he defended the war: "Finally, we've got a just war."

---

1   Author's translation; only published in Hebrew, *Haaretz*, July 21, 2006.

At that time, there were already hundreds of thousands of Lebanese refugees; villages and cities had been bombed, with many killed in the name of "justice." The brutality of that war did not suddenly emerge. It developed over a period of many years, sometimes far from the eyes of the world media. Here is part of an interview with Yehoshua which was conducted in the spring of 2004, prior to the publication of his book *Mission of the Human Resource Man* (the italic parts in the following text appeared only in the Hebrew version of the article; the English editors of *Haaretz* chose not to include these parts in their own version of this interview):

It's possible that there will be a war with the Palestinians. It's not necessary, it's not impossible. But if there is a war, it will be a very short one. Maybe a war of six days. Because after we remove the settlements and after we stop being an occupation army, *all the rules of war will be different*. We will exercise our full force. We will not have to run around looking for this terrorist or that instigator—*we will make use of force against an entire population*. We will use total force. Because from the minute we withdraw *I don't even want to know their names. I don't want any personal relations with them*. I am no longer in a situation of occupation and policing and B'Tselem [the human rights organization]. Instead, I will be standing opposite them in a position of nation versus nation. State versus state. I am not going to perpetrate war crimes for their own sake, but I will use all my force against them. If there is shooting at Ashkelon, there is no electricity in Gaza. We shall use force against an entire population. We shall use total force. It will be a totally different war. It will be much harder on the Palestinians. If they shoot Qassam missiles at Ashkelon, we will cut electricity to Gaza. We shall cut communications in Gaza. We shall prevent fuel from entering Gaza. We will use our full force as we did on the Egyptian [Suez] Canal in 1969. And then, when the Palestinian suffering will be totally different, much more serious, they will, by themselves, eliminate the terror. The Palestinian nation will overcome terrorism itself. It won't have any other choice. Let them stop the shooting. No matter if it is the PA [Palestinian Authority] or the Hamas. Whoever takes responsibility for the fuel, electricity and hospitals, and sees that they do not function, will operate within a few days to stop the shooting of the Qassams. This new situation will totally change the rules of the game. Not a desired war, but definitely a purifying one. A war that will make it clear to the Palestinians that they are sovereign. The suffering they will go through in the post-occupation situation will make clear to them that they must stop the violence, because now they are sovereign. From the moment we retreat I don't want to know their names at all. I don't want any personal relationship with them, and I am not going to commit war crimes for their own sake.[2]

Note this short sentence: "We will not have to run around looking for this terrorist or that instigator." In March 2004, when the interview was conducted, the systematic killing of intifada activists in the occupied territories had reached the proportions of daily manhunts—with jails and prisons crammed full, detention camps crowded, long lines of Palestinians stuck at IDF checkpoints for many hours, and the IDF indiscriminately killing what it called "terrorists en route to attacks in Israel," which was actually a systematic expansion of the activity of its death squads. But it is important for me to consider the terrorist logic of the strategist A. B. Yehoshua: "they" fire a Qassam (who are "they"?) and "we" stop the flow of electricity to them (who are "them"?). How easy it is to shut off electricity for the infants of Gaza! How simple

---

2 "A nation that knows no bounds," *Haaretz*, interview with A. B. Yehoshua, March 18, 2004.

to deplete the fuel in Gaza's hospitals and in its water pumps, "because they fire a Qassam"! This is terrorist logic par excellence.

When the IDF shut off the electricity in Gaza in June 2006, and when Ehud Olmert said in his characteristically boorish way, "Dialysis patients don't die from this," the systematic shut-off of electricity was the implementation of a plan A. B. Yehoshua had proposed. This is how an intellectual can kill. Yehoshua did not invent this sadism, nor did the Israeli radio listeners who called in demanding the cutting off the water to "them" or that "they" should be bombed or massacred. Neither the "people" nor the writer, "a member of the peace camp," had invented this. The IDF had already committed such crimes in the past, for example the mass starvation techniques during the first intifada, the cutting off of electricity in Beirut back in the winter of 1998, and previous bombings of many population centers, including all of the Egyptian canal cities. Nonetheless, even in this context, it is worth noting the climax of the interview with A. B. Yehoshua in 2004: "Not a desired war, but definitely a purifying one. A war that will make it clear to the Palestinians that they are sovereign." Would I be wrong to suggest that this is a fascistic text?

It is worth noting the ease with which people like A. B. Yehoshua are sold in the Western market as "peaceniks."

In Italy, for reasons that we cannot go into here, this took on the most grotesque form. While those attending A. B. Yehoshua's lecture at Tel Aviv University were handed copies of the interview by protesting left-wing academics, the author received the Naples peace prize along with with Tariq Ali from Britain.

On September 1, 2000, on the very eve of the second intifada, Dutch television broadcast a dialogue between Yehoshua and the Palestinian writer and filmmaker from Ramallah Liana Bader. Yehoshua was introduced as "a peace activist who is almost persecuted in Israel for being a leftist." He spoke with an increasing tone of superiority toward Bader, who complained about Palestinian distress during the Oslo era. Here is how Yehoshua preached to her:

> Now I am really angry, I am really angry because you are not being fair. There was an intifada here and every day a Palestinian was wounded and there were Israelis wounded too; there was war all the time. It's been three or four years now without terror. Everything is calm, there are no demonstrations, maybe just here and there, but less. So you can't say that the situation is the same. There is improvement ...

Bader argued:

> I have no state, I have no security and all around me
> my land is being constantly robbed—

Yehoshua interrupted her:

> Don't pretend to be more wretched than you really
> are. You have problems but …

Bader tried to finish the sentence she had started, but
Yehoshua continued instead:

> You have your own police, you already have a kind
> of an army. When I come to Ramallah I see the
> Palestinian policemen sitting with their AK-47 guns,
> and so on. You have Arafat, who is received all over
> the world like a prime minister …[3]

Four years later, after the death of Arafat, Yehoshua told
Tel Aviv's *Time Out*:

> Arafat was a symbol of the refugees and the right
> of return. He was a chaotic person, an essentially

---

3 "The dead should be counted," from an interview on Dutch TV, December 10,
2000, *Ha'it*.

powerless leader, without a police and without a
mechanism for subjugation, who ruled by virtue of
his authoritativeness ... only the chaos of the eternal
refugee, and he drew his entire people into this.[4]

The gap between the two interviews should not mislead us.
In both cases, there is profound and consistent animosity
toward Palestinian suffering; in both, there is contempt
for the weak, for the victim. Luckily, Yehoshua does not
write with ease. In newspapers, he prefers interviews.
But in the interviews he talks a lot, eager to win over the
interviewer; he enjoys pontificating with arms flailing,
thereby uttering a great many interesting truths.

"Israelization"

Most symptomatic in Yehoshua's outbursts—in Israel, in
Hebrew, absolutely not in Europe—is his attitude toward
the Arabs within the State of Israel. The Palestinian
presence in Israel bothers him, as it does many Israeli
politicians. About 20 percent of the citizens of Israel within
the old borders are Palestinians, who are entitled to vote
for the Knesset. The harsh discrimination against them is
reflected in the budgets for education, sanitation, health

---

4   *Time Out* (Tel Aviv), November 11, 2004.

and welfare; the constitutional discrimination against them is expressed primarily in land legislation, including a prohibition on them owning water resources and 80 percent of the land. He does not join the fascistic calls by politicians on the right to expel the Arabs from Israel, but he is troubled by the fact that the Arabs in Israel regard themselves as belonging to the Palestinian people. Back in 1986, in a debate conducted in the newspapers, he called upon the writer Anton Shammas to pack up his belongings and leave the country, the birthplace of Shammas and his forefathers. Regarding the events of October 2000, when the police killed thirteen demonstrators in the streets and in the city squares, the author, "a member of the peace camp," said the following to an Arab newspaper from the Galilee (in December 2001):

> We, as Jews in the state, face a real problem, and it is how to work toward achieving the Israelization of the Arabs. And I believe that it is the duty of all of us, Right and Left and all the rest, to take action in order to achieve this goal, even if this happens in stages.[5]

I will skip over a great many political issues in order to

---

5   *Kul al-arab*, December 28, 2001.

reach the main point regarding Yehoshua: the wish that there should not be Arabs among us or that they should become a part of us ("Israelization") is an element of Yehoshua's great fear of ethnic heterogeneity. This fear is the real axis of the novel *The Liberated Bride*, the most racist Hebrew novel written in recent years. The Arabs of Israel are not Palestinians in this novel. When they act like Palestinians, they are traitors or imbeciles. The Arabs of Israel are mainly represented as serene villagers who have no interest in politics. They are pleasant natives, sometimes a bit devious, sycophantic and especially ugly. The main effort of this novel is devoted to describing the Palestinians in the West Bank as buffoons. The disparagement of Mahmoud Darwish and his poetry is remarkable, together with ridicule of the Palestinians' longings for their olive trees, and for their tragedy. Here too we must recall that no one spoiled the European celebration of the book. Even what used to be the Italian Communists fell in line with European liberalism. The hatred for immigrants and for the East requires an Israeli advocate.

From Molcho to Rivlin

In my view, Yehoshua has written one good novel: *Molcho* (published in English as *Five Seasons*). He experienced a period of grace when he mourned the death of his

136

father, with feelings of guilt about his long disavowal of his ethnic origins, and also with the "discovery of the Mizrahim [Sephardim]" in Israeli society (since the elections in 1981). The novel centers around Molcho, a Mizrahi Jew from Jerusalem, who lives in the "European" Carmel section of Haifa and whose wife, of German origin (German always has the "most European" connotation in Israeli literature), has just died. Upon the death of his Ashkenazi wife, he has lost all of his powers of discrimination between good and bad—that is, between "positive European" (classical music) and "negative Mizrahi" (noisy music)—and has been left between two worlds. He wanders around "Europe" (Haifa's Carmel or Paris or Berlin), and Mizrahi Israel (Jerusalem) but does not feel at home. Indeed, there is much evidence in the book of the author's loathing of Sephardism, revealed particularly through memories of his deceased wife. (For example, she forced the protagonist to bathe regularly, something he was unaccustomed to doing as a Mizrahi, of course.) *The Liberated Bride*, on the other hand, written over fifteen years later, is a bad novel. It was written when Yehoshua was already an author who was more or less well known in the West, against the background of the growing enmity toward Muslims in Europe. Here the border does not run through the hero, but rather the hero forcibly marks the border.

137

Yehoshua, as we know, comes from a Sephardi/Mizrahi home and was born in Jerusalem in the 1930s. One can find many connections between the "author's self" in *Molcho* and in *The Liberated Bride*. For example, just as Molcho's Ashkenazi wife orders her Sephardi husband to bathe regularly, Rivlin's wife insists that her husband wash himself before she consents to sleep with him because he still smells of the Arab village they visited earlier in the evening. In the racist novel, the narrating subject pretends to be a complete Ashkenazi—that is, a European. Indeed, going to a concert is part of a regular cultural menu. But the primary Freudian slip can be found, of course, in the name of the hero in both of the novels. Molcho is a typical Sephardic Jerusalemite family name dating from pre-Zionist Palestine, like the name Mani (the title of another of Yehoshua's novels). Both of the names, like both of the protagonists, belong to the world of symbols through which Yehoshua sought to contend with his Sephardic past.

On the other hand, Rivlin, the hero of *The Liberated Bride*, is the most familiar name of the Ashkenazim from the pre-Zionist Jerusalem community.[6] There are very few quintessentially Ashkenazi Jerusalemite names from

---

6   Yehoshua was embarrassed when this slip of the pen was noted in the reviews of *The Liberated Bride* (New York, 2003). In his next novel, *The Mission of the Human Resource Man* (published in English as *A Woman in Jerusalem*, New York, 2006), he did not give his protagonist a name, and thus got around the need to define his ethnic origin.

the century that preceded Zionism, and Rivlin, the name of one of the largest and more well-known families in politics, culture and business, is one. In short, the autobiographical hero has traveled the entire route from "the confession of weakness" of a Mizrahi Jew through to his transformation into the opposite: a learned expert on Middle Eastern affairs, married to a judge and primarily "culturally minded." Yehoshua was unable to choose caution and a less transparent name that would have hidden somewhat his desire to resemble the Ashkenazi neighbor from the next street in Jerusalem. As in the interviews, here too Yehoshua forgot himself, in this case because of a violent desire in this case to wipe out the past, to transform Molcho the Sephardi into Rivlin the Ashkenazi.

When engaging with A. B. Yehoshua's literature, and particularly when considering the way in which he tries to contend with his Mizrahi origin, it is important to note the place where Yehoshua builds the "we." His "I" can only define itself in relation to an "us." But "we," of course, requires a "they" in order to become an "us," in order to become an "I." Yehoshua does not succeed in finding for himself the collective that contains "I" other than an "Israeliness" that eliminates all traces of his foreignness. Here is what Yehoshua wrote in the late 1980s about his childhood in Jerusalem on the eve of the establishment of the state, a childhood that included friends from the Scouts movement (Ashkenazim) and studies at the Gymnasia Rehavia high school (Ashkenazi), as well as his place of origin—a place he had to reject when he wanted to become an Israeli:

> The old Sephardim, the family elders and so on, were only part of my experience and not a part that elicited much identification. Other heroes emerged during the years of preparation for establishing the state, and I watched for many hours from the window of my home on King George Street [Jerusalem's main street] as they walked by the Talor cinema and Histadrut building ... They were not connected to my grandfather, who strolled in his black robe and tarbush along the streets of Jerusalem. When occasionally encountering him on the street while walking with my friend from the Hebrew Gymnasium, I would feel somewhat confused and embarrassed.[7]

Here one can see how well he knows that there is no definition for Israeliness that does not include the Ashkenazi and the non-Ashkenazi. Israeliness does not neutralize the citizen's "previous" ethnic origin, but takes the previous origin as a starting point.

---

7   A. B. Yehoshua, "The Wall and the Mountain," Tel Aviv, 1990, p. 223.

In the same article, Yehoshua outlines his Zionist fantasy:

> I did not want to be Ashkenazi, but rather Israeli. And this was a good, moral and correct ideological objective from all perspectives. But—to be completely honest with myself—this also included a type of comfort, particularly in distinguishing myself from the waves of immigration of Jews from Arab countries who arrived in the early 1950s with all of their problems.[8]

Nearly fifteen years after writing this article, in an interview in March 2004, without changing the wording very much, Yehoshua tried to update his formulation regarding the unhealed wound of his "shameful" Sephardic origin. Responding to the interviewer's questions, he complained of discrimination:

> No one ever came to S. Yizhar [the doyen of Israeli writers] with questions about his family's Russian past. What I'm saying is that there is a tacit assumption here that if you come from a weak minority you are not supposed to leave it. You mustn't betray it. Well, I don't accept that. I simply don't accept it. Ever

---

8   Ibid., p. 232.

since I can remember, my desire was entirely turned
towards the Israeli way of life.[9]

With regard to this source of suffering, Yehoshua insists on
writing again and again a fantasy of a neutral Israeliness,
devoid of roots. Only within the Israeli fantasy will he no
longer be ashamed of the origins that trouble him. It is
not a simple matter for an author to bear the memory of
his Moroccan mother, the memory of his Arabic-speaking
father and grandfather, with their distinct Mizrahi accent,
and still to hate the Mizrah (the East). On the other hand,
not everyone translates this enmity into literary form,
and not every author turns the pain into racist hatred,
while identifying with the state and, beyond it, with
the "superiority of the West." But Yehoshua does. His
entire intellectual path is characterized by a rejection of
the wedge that divides East and West within the Jewish
people.

We should cite this painful point, which portrays "the
Israeli experience" as the place where everyone strips
off his/her "previous" identity and dons a "new identity,"
as the point of departure of "The Sorrows of Yehoshua."
This Yehoshua—who takes pains to emphasize here that
"I did not think that I have some sort of special mission

---

9   "A nation that knows no bounds," *Haaretz*.

and special responsibility in regard to my group of ethnic origin"—definitely believes that he has a "special mission and special responsibility" with regard to the group to which he is seeking to appeal. All of his public appearances are imbued with a sense of mission pertaining to the target group—that is, "Israeli identity"—which is nothing more than Ashkenazism that covers up the "embarrassing" past. Note the "proof" of the new experience, which is ostensibly neither Mizrahi nor Ashkenazi:

> My sister and I do not have a Mizrahi accent. My father and mother had a Mizrahi accent. If you think about it, this is quite an amazing thing: A one-year-old child realizes that he should adopt the general Israeli accent and not the specific Mizrahi accent. That the source of his identity will not be the family and home; instead, the source of identity will be the majority, the friend, the school. This is at the most preliminary stage of all. It is as if the home itself says: Don't behave as you would at home. Be like the teachers. Be like the children in the kindergarten. Don't be like father and mother.[10]

---

10   Ibid.

The "general Israeli" accent is first of all an Ashkenazi accent or, better, a non-Mizrahi accent. A large part of "Israeliness" uses Mizrahism as a negative definition, as material for jokes and entertainment, just as in many countries where the folklore of the margins, of the groups that are distant from the center, is mobilized. Yehoshua's denial of or embarrassment at his ethnic origin through the representation of "a general accent" also certainly appears in many cultures. In every culture that has a linguistic and cultural hierarchy, it is embarrassing to belong to the lower rungs. However, the transition in Israel from "Oriental" to "general" is a transition from life in the Middle East to the Western fantasy of Israeliness. This is the swamp in which Yehoshua's self-hatred developed. It is not detached for even a moment from the ideological developments around it. Yehoshua, of course, is not the only person who finds in the Zionist enterprise a Western refuge from Mizrahi origin, nor is he the only person who finds in hatred of Arabs the chance to "forget" the ethnic barrier between the Jews. Anyone seeking to explain the Likud phenomenon of anti-Arab Mizrahim can plumb this particular swamp.

However, unlike so many others, Yehoshua made himself into the trumpeter of the denial process. Even in the previous quotation—which almost reflects some understanding of spoken language (for what is an "accent" other than spoken language?) versus the language of literature—he brandishes the "modernity" of his existence for as far back as he can remember. He refuses to understand what underlies denial of the accent learned at his mother's bosom, that of her lullabies. He fails to see the manner in which children, in general, are exiled from the speech of their parents, whether with the help of their parents or despite their parents, and are led by the state and education system to believe that high culture, that of the university, let's say, or that of the dazzling theater lights, is the real culture, as opposed to the culture of the child's everyday surroundings. He chooses not to grasp what happens to someone who finds refuge very far from his father's home and opts for another symbolic father who is different from him, such as the state, or the Ashkenazi. Instead of all this, Yehoshua aggressively and bitterly repels any criticism. I preach Zionism, Yehoshua says in essence, on behalf of the general interest, while you all ask me about the interests of the minority. But he hates minorities because he does not want to number among them. Fifteen years before he addressed the lost accent of his mother in an interview in *Haaretz*, Yehoshua explained these things, this exile, in a more resolute way:

During our childhood and adolescence, the heroes [my father] presented to us were not actually the Sephardi rabbi or notables of the [Sephardi] community, but rather the top Jewish officials in the government offices of the British Mandate where he worked, scholars of the Hebrew University, where he completed his high school studies when he was in his early twenties. Those were his real favorites and he would speak excitedly about them.[11]

That is, his father had already undergone this colonial experience: to be a child from old Jerusalem, to grow up among Arabs and Mizrahi Jews, and to regard the Ashkenazim who arrived from Europe as the model.

This is not only Yehoshua's trauma. This is the trauma of so many Mizrahi Jews in Israel: their denial of their ethnic origins always entails a distinction between East and West within Israeli life. In order to cope with the trauma, and in complete identification with the ideological directives of the state, Yehoshua identifies himself with the West:

I think the process was correct. It was correct to repress, it was correct to pour a new concrete floor of a new identity. I think the Mizrahim who undertook this process benefited from it. It was healthy for them and healthy for the culture. Look at [Mizrahi politicians]

---

11   Yehoshua, "The Wall and the Mountain," p. 232.

Nissim Zvili, Amir Peretz, [Mizrahi writer] Eli Amir. On the other hand, the Mizrahim who were unable to repress remained with the bitterness of [the religious party] Shas. They were left with no alternative other than to return to the influence of religion.[12]

Was it really "correct to repress?" Is Amir Peretz proof of non-repression? Is the writer Eli Amir the proof of the correctness of this path? Is A. B. Yehoshu himself proof? Why should one repress anything at all? Would it not have been possible to migrate to Israel and preserve one's identity, like the Jewish immigrant from Galicia? Apparently not, for it is not the same immigration: the immigration of Yehoshua and of the Mizrahim in Israel includes the shame of being Oriental. Yehoshua is not only at issue here, but rather the masses of Mizrahim who have always been placed in the same impossible position. Our subject here is, ultimately, the hatred toward Arabs that appears among the Mizrahim in Israel. It is different from the Western scorn; it takes upon itself the obligation of proving this hatred. (Moreover, can a writer repress without paying a price in brutality, not only in brutality toward himself, but also in the brutality cited extensively at the beginning of this chapter?)

---

12 "A nation that knows no bounds," *Haaretz*.

Is the "Israeli" experience both non-Mizrahi and non-Ashkenazi? Not at all. There is no clearer way that the erroneousness of this idea is manifested than in the opposition that Yehoshua himself builds here between, on the one hand, modernity—that is, identification with the Ashkenazi model—and, on the other hand, Shas. Other possibilities, such as the Black Panthers or the Mizrahi Democratic Rainbow—that is, the political expression of Israeli Mizrahism, the possibility of facing up politically to the Mizrahi situation—do not even occur to him.

The Liberated Bride by Yehoshua and *A Tale of Love and Darkness* by Amos Oz were published at about the same time. Oz wrote an autobiography that was, of course, also a biography of the Jewish people in Israel and of Zionism: he became the people and the people became him. The book stirred up great excitement in Israel. Everyone could identify themselves there—their attitudes, or the attitude of the Yishuv (the pre-1948 Jewish residents) toward the Holocaust, their attitudes toward Agnon and Germany—all within the narcissistic framework of the *imaginaire*. But Yehoshua is not capable of writing such an autobiography, precisely for the reasons described here. His autobiography pits him against the Israeli "collective self" whose ethnic origin is always, in every story, to be found in Eastern Europe. The autobiography places Amos Oz within the "collective self." Does Yehoshua develop a different poetic art because of this inability? Is he ready to write something that does not invite narcissistic identification with "the writer who is the people"? He cannot do this, except by exchanging the Mizrahi Molcho with the Middle East expert Rivlin, and of course with belligerence toward the Arab minority.

To Be a Mizrahi in Israel

At the beginning, the division between Mizrahim and Ashkenazim in Israel was not even a cultural divide; at the beginning, it was not a divide of wealth and poverty (though the Mizrahim became a majority among the impoverished Jews in Israel, as well as among the prison population and the Jewish proletariat in Israel); it was not a division of skin color or of biology (despite references to "blacks"). The division between Mizrahim and Ashkenazim was not a divide over anything "natural" or "cultural." Prior to anything else, it was a political division—that is, a division instituted by the state. It is impossible to think of this division prior to the creation of the Jewish state, or before the manifestation of Zionism in the heart of the Middle East. Despite the fact that there were Sephardi and Ashkenazi Jews in the country before Zionism—in Jerusalem, in Tiberias, in Hebron— there was no nationalist or cultural dimension to the relations between them, no links of "a shared past," or of "a common language." At most, there were religious connections between them. And this aspect was also problematic from the outset.

In the long process of establishing the state, from the start of Zionist settlement in Palestine and with greater intensity after the official birth of the state in 1948, the category of the "Mizrahi" was created.[13] There is nothing "natural" or "cultural" that connects the Jews of Yemen with the Jews of Egypt, or Libyan Jewry with Iranian Jewry, or the Jews of Kurdistan with the Jews of North Africa—except for the connection the state created between them as Jews from Arab or Muslim lands living in a state defined as Jewish (that is, in struggle against the Arabs or the East [*Mizrah*]). Those defined as Mizrahim in the new collective (and this was recorded for years in the state's official statistics under the rubric of country of origin and in statistical summaries of "immigrants from Asia and Africa") were, until they arrived and until becoming "Mizrahim," part of Arab or Muslim society

---

13 Yehoshua says touching things in an interview about the creation of the Mizrahi, without realizing that he is speaking about the very creation of this category: "And my mother, who arrived at age 16 from Morocco, was completely foreign in Jerusalem. She did not live the Ashkenazi context or the Sephardi. Thus, she directed me and my sister toward the Israeli experience. She more or less told us from a very early age to venture outside, into the dynamic Israel. Not to live the life of the weak minority but rather to go to the majority. To the hegemonic." ("A nation that knows no bounds," *Haaretz*).

and/or a religious minority within Muslim society, but definitely not "Mizrahim." They only became "Mizrahim" after the creation of the Jewish political entity, which defined them within an older colonial discourse—that is, in line with the prevailing division in the Western world: East (Islam) versus West (and Christianity).

Let me state this more clearly. From the moment the state and/or Zionism placed the challenge of nationalism before all of the Jews, to change from a religion into a nation, the Jews who came from the lands of Asia and Africa were compelled—whether they were forced or tempted to come, whether they did so willingly or for lack of any other alternative, and even when they were motivated by messianic fervor—to undergo a double migration. One migration was to become "Mizrahim"— that is, to receive the common denomination of "non-Ashkenazi"—Persians and Moroccans, Kurds and Egyptians. The second migration was immediately, in the same process, to alienate themselves from their "shared origins" (Jews from Arab lands, or from the lands of Islam) and be part of "Israeliness"—that is, to receive a new identity that was constructed around a hegemonic Ashkenazi standard. When Yehoshua complains, "After all, if you are Polish, no one demands that you remain loyal to Polishness. No one came to Yizhar with questions about the Russian past of his family," he arrives at the right place. But, as is the tendency with deniers, he immediately flees. The "Israeliness" Yehoshua speaks of with such enthusiasm is not a new site, unconnected to the past or place of origin. It is a great illusion. This is what he says in an interview with *Haaretz*:

> When grandfather walked along the street, it was strange. I had to explain it. Understand, I was a minority. And as a minority, I had to make sure that they would not categorize me. This became particularly acute in the 1950s, when the mass immigration arrived, when all of those new Mizrahim came. There was a real threat then that I would be swept into the Moroccan wave.[14]

It is true that some of the Ashkenazim, particular the religious ones, experienced a violent migration, including "modernization," and were compelled in the worst case to become a new Jew. But, as we have noted, in contrast to the Ashkenazim the Jews from the Arab and Muslim countries underwent two migrations: one in their redefinition as "Mizrahim," unequal "foreigners in the new culture," and the second in at the same time being forced to tragically renounce their non-Ashkenazi

---

14   "A nation that knows no bounds," *Haaretz*.

identity in favor of "Israeliness." Yehoshua shattered this
illusion in *Molcho* in a very poetic way. But since *Molcho*,
he has been selling the illusion with a growing measure of
arrogance, particularly after discovering how thirsty the
Europeans are for this type of panegyric for modernization
and reproach toward the East.

Yehoshua's case provides us with a good perspective for
thinking about Israel. It is impossible to think about the
State of Israel without thinking about the border between
East and West, which all of the Mizrahim experience
within themselves, in the everyday interpellation by the
hegemonic powers (the education system, the radio,
the television): "Don't be from the East!" This gaping
wound is expressed in the Mizrahi complaints about
discrimin-ation, in "subversive folklore," in anti-
Ashkenazi curses of the worst type ("Why didn't they
kill you all in Auschwitz?" was particularly popular at
one point), in thousands of cultural decisions such as
"returning to tradition," especially among the common
folk, in maintaining a "Mizrahi accent," in Jerusalem, in
the towns populated by North African Jewry (where the
third generation of immigrants still preserve a certain
Moroccan accent). But this wound—the State of Israel—
defines the Mizrahi majority as a minority precisely in the
way that Yehoshua explains so well in an interview that
seeks to justify the "positive repression": the Mizrahim

always have to "meet the standard"—"modernity," manners, classical music, volunteering for a combat unit in the army, excellence in studies, or, in Yehoshua's simple language, "to be like Amir Peretz."

The Likud party, like other political parties fed by hatred, learned how to offer the masses of Mizrahim a clearer border than the Zionist Left offered: The border between the East and the West runs between the Jews and the Arabs clear and simple, according to Likud. It is true that the Zionist Left acted in precisely the same way, as with the settlement of thousands of immigrants from Arab lands after 1948 in neighborhoods and villages that had just been emptied of their Palestinian owners and were located adjacent to the next lines of confrontation. However, Likud was not implicated in the "Mizrahization" of the immigrants—that is, their designation as Mizrahim; after all, the Zionist Left had been responsible for bringing them in, for "modernizing," Westernizing them. Likud offered them the possibility of "fleeing from Mizrahism" and becoming Israelis by hating Arabs. The Zionist Left was "the state" in this structure, the painful cleavage between East and West. The Likud, in this structure, is "the people of Israel" or "the new state" it will establish one day, after it gets rid of the Arabs, or the "elites," or the Left, or all of them. This is the messianic message Likud sold to its miserable voters, together with the destruction of the welfare state. Whoever fails to understand the failure of the attempt by the Zionist Left (Peace Now, for example) to dig a political ditch between the settlers and the Mizrahim does not understand the extent to which colonization in the occupied territories (that is, the escalation of the conflict) expedited the formation of the new "people of Israel" in which Mizrahism serves as a type of extreme patriotism. As the conflict with the Palestinians intensifies to the point of no return, the Arab East moves further eastward, and the Jews, all of them, can find themselves in the West in the end. This is exactly what happens in Yehoshua's novel *The Liberated Bride*, a song of praise for the separation wall.

After he wrote *Molcho* and confessed his weakness for a moment, Yehoshua made every effort to shift the border running within the non-Ashkenazi Israeli, his Molcho, to other places so that the Mizrahi Jews in his imaginary world would be "Western." *Mr. Mani* was another such biological attempt (according to which the Jews were always a "mix" of Mizrahim and Ashkenazim, but the final product is Western). *Voyage to the End of the Millennium* is a "cultural" attempt, according to which the Jews already disengaged from the East a thousand years ago when they accepted the modern European prohibition on polygamy, unlike the Muslims. And thus, against the background of Paris in the early Middle Ages, a false and completely ahistorical portrayal was built of an alliance between monogamous Parisian Christians and Jews from Morocco versus the polygamous Muslims—that is, the Arabs.

Yehoshua needs the separation wall because only "separation"—that is, a clear demarcation of "outside" and "inside"—gives him a sense that a "uniform identity" is indeed being created. Anyone who takes the trouble to study *The Liberated Bride* will find the Middle East expert Rivlin scribbling a hackneyed thesis on the civil war in Algeria, which supposedly erupted due to "a medley of tongues." (To strengthen his argument, Yehoshua revealed that he took this imagined academic thesis from a real article by an Algerian journalist, who wrote about "linguistic unity.") This novel enabled Yehoshua to finally come out of the closet. Here he moved the border to its "final" place: The East is the Palestinian and the Jew is part of the West. "I don't even want to know their names," Yehoshua said in the July 2006 interview. As in the most terrible Jewish curse: May their names be obliterated.

V

In Lieu of a Conclusion: A Banished Thought from the East about a Polish Saltfish

In Hanoch Levin's play *Those Who Walk in the Darkness*, the protagonists' thoughts converse with each other. One of them is Herring Thought and the other is Ass Thought. Both speak about the material lives of the Ass and of the Herring (an apparent allusion to the food of poor East European Jews in Israel). Only then the Narrator declares:

> THE NARRATOR: In the streets of our town lately wanders another thought, abstract, very complex, the latest word in post-modern theory, a disciple of the aged French professor Lazhan.
>
> She is beautiful, daring, delicate, heavenly; in Paris, young female students, beneath their straight, lush hair, think of her during the autumn nights ...
> *[Ass Thought and Herring Thought approach her]*

ASS THOUGHT: I desire so to cling to you, sometimes the throat chokes, sometimes you want to
rise above simplicity and crudeness, to forget the
flesh, to penetrate higher spheres.

Sometimes you aspire, but lack the strength
to acquire; my wonderful, spiritual, airy, slender
one! ...

HERRING THOUGHT: A herring, what is there to
say, is merely a herring, and yet, I allow myself
to ... I'm not saying, after all I come from the
lower classes ... and yet ... one reeks of fish but
the heart seeks the horizon ... I just thought what
a wonderful match we could have been, me and
you, saltfish and spirit, post-modernism and kip-
per, you and I! ...

LAZHAN THOUGHT: Who are you? I'm from the Sor-
bonne!

ASS THOUGHT: I'm from the underwear drawer.

HERRING THOUGHT: I'm from the barrel.[1]

At first, I intended to conclude this book with an essay
on the playwright and author Hanoch Levin. I am told
that readers outside Israel are completely unfamiliar with

---

1   Extracts from Hanoch Levin's *Those Who Walk in the Darkness* are from the
unpublished English translation by Shir Freibach, *They Who Walk in the Dark: A
Nocturnal Vision*.

Hanoch Levin. So why do I give up this original intention? Precisely because I have read Hanoch Levin attentively and have understood his lesson that our fantasy about the West is a hopeless fantasy. Indeed, we will never be there, will not truly exist there—that is, with you, really—unless we don a Western mask, adopt your discourse, your standards. This is more or less what the Hebrew literature that is familiar in the West does. I also indirectly spoke about this in previous chapters.

The matter is ostensibly simple. The Israeli fantasy of the West presumes a norm: "The standards for universalism, beauty, the good reside among you in the West—in Paris, in London, in Los Angeles. We would like to live there, but only by living here can we fantasize about the life there." This, of course, is wonderful material for comedy. However, this comedy says something different to the Western reader or audience: The Jew remains "different"—even the Israeli, Ashkenazi or Sephardi, right-wing or left-wing—does not really belong to the West. But your standards too, dear Western reader, the standards based on the assumption that the good and the beautiful are Western, are also re-examined in Hanoch Levin's comedies. This is what I had planned to discuss in my final chapter, based on a serious analysis of Levin's comedy.

So let us satisfy ourselves with a simple summary of what is relevant to this book, perhaps to the next book, or perhaps to what I can write only for a Hebrew readership. And it will be easily understood by most readers of Hebrew literature simply because the problematic "Western fantasy" in Israeli life, in Jewish life, is so fragile and collapses so easily. This is the topic on which Hanoch Levin became so effective and also so infuriating in Israel, while this perhaps also denied him any chance of success in the West. The West asks our writers to represent a "collective." But real writers are not ambassadors.

With Levin, the Western fantasy does not fit the Western fantasy of the dominant ideology in Israel (let's call it Israeli Zionism). This ideology assumes that for us, the Jews, complete normality is only in Israel, far from the West. But the normality also assumes that the "normal," the standard for normality, can only be found in the West. Within this context, the new Jew of the West appears, a type of Paul Newman from *Exodus*.

There is a politics of translation—exemplified by the fact that most of those who read literature translated from Hebrew have never heard of our most important playwright, who is certainly greater than the writers who are translated with such fanfare in the capitals of the West.

This is because the politics of translation from Hebrew to French or to English or to German is not random and also does not operate autonomously. No order operates on its own, as if there were no agents, as if there were no embassy, as if there were no Institute for the Translation of Hebrew Literature, as if there were no cultural attachés. Moreover, and here we return to what we discussed in earlier chapters, the Western demand for foreign literature is also not a matter of a "universal cultural necessity" or a "search for quality literature," but is rather inscribed into a market economy and a particular type of cultural consumption. This question should also be asked in other ways: How is it that Israeli writers have succeeded in garnering good sales figures abroad? Were they proclaimed "universal authors" or only "Israeli authors"? What did they give up in their writing? What did they cover up? To what extent did they respond to the Western demand for the new Jew? It bears repeating: It is impossible to review the dozens of articles in the French press about Amos Oz's *A Tale of Love and Darkness*, for example, without noting how all of them, without a single exception, duplicate precisely the same thing. Rather than turning on a discussion of the book, the articles focus on the character of the author as the embodiment of Israeli Jewish history. I am not speaking about the power of major publishers to sell books like bras or a new cellphone, but rather about the need this campaign seeks to satisfy, a need I have already discussed as the Return of the Colonial, or the Holocaust as a Western "hit," or "the new Jew."

No culture exists "for itself," and a foreign culture

certainly does not exist without the iconography that mediates between the metropolis and itself. This is a ponderous matter and should be addressed separately. Levin, of course, never gave up the desire to be published abroad and, on the other hand, he never denied the difference between "here" and "there." On the contrary.

Here, what better conclusion could there be for this book than another extract from the play I cited earlier?

LAZHAN THOUGHT: I hang around Luxembourg and Saint Germain, sit in Café de Flore and Brasserie Lipp, sleep at the Hôtel Passy, will die in Neuilly, and will be buried in Père Lachaise. And you?
ASS THOUGHT: We live in the gutter …
HERRING THOUGHT: And will be buried in the sewer …
ASS THOUGHT: But dreaming of Paris.

Later, Herring Thought delivers its summary of life "here" and "there":

HERRING THOUGHT: And the herring is forgotten. I will never get to penetrate French culture, I shall never be welcomed in the household, I will only peek around the door with yearning eyes turn around and return to my homeland, to be what I am: a banished thought from the East about a Polish saltfish.